16–19

Changes in Education
and Training

16–19

Changes in Education
and Training

Edited by
Tom Whiteside, Alan Sutton and Tim Everton

David Fulton Publishers
London

David Fulton Publishers Ltd
2 Barbon Close, London WC1N 3JX

First published in Great Britain by
David Fulton Publishers 1992

British Library Cataloguing in Publication Data

A catalogue record for this book is available from the British Library

ISBN 1-85346-204-7

Typeset by Spectrum Typesetting Ltd. London
Printed in Great Britain by BPCC Wheatons Ltd, Exeter

Contents

List of Contributors

Michael Clegg	Principal, Preston College
Graham Conway	Coordinator, Leicester City Cluster, Leicestershire LEA
Derek D'Hooghe	Assistant Director of Education, Leicestershire Local Education Authority
Tim Everton	Vice-Principal, Homerton College, Cambridge
Paul Kennewell	Flexible Learning Coordinator, Northamptonshire TVEI
David Kerr	Lecturer, University of Leicester School of Education
Louise Kidd	Principal, Rutland Sixth Form College
Tony Lawson	Lecturer in Education, University of Leicester School of Education
Malcolm Maguire	Co-Director, Centre for Labour Market Studies, University of Leicester
Peter Mayne	Vice-Principal, Rutland Sixth Form College
Neil Stock	Coordinator, Leicester City Cluster, Leicestershire LEA
Alan Sutton	Lecturer, University of Leicester School of Education
Tom Whiteside	Senior Lecturer in Education, University of Leicester School of Education

INTRODUCTION

England and Wales have a unique system of 16–19 education and training, characterized by features which have proved major obstacles to reform and which are seen as inextricably linked to the low levels of participation and attainment of students who remain in full time education and training post-16. These features include a rigid academic/vocational divide, a stratified and hierarchical qualification system, a persistent view of the inherent superiority of academic qualifications and the lack of status of alternative vocational qualifications.

Critics have argued that there has been a long-standing failure to implement a coherent policy of education and training for this age group. Previous attempts at reform have tended to be *ad hoc*, incremental and as much motivated by political expediency as by a recognition of the need for large scale reform. Such attempts have frequently foundered on the strength of conservative forces, particularly from those who have progressed through the system and now hold influential positions in the DES, the public schools and the universities.

Current policy in this area continues to be disjointed and inconsistent. However over the last decade there has been mounting pressure for a major re-appraisal of the provision of education and training for this age group. A loose 'alliance' (including, amongst others, the CBI and the TUC, with support from groupings within the Department of Employment and the Department of Trade and Industry and from professional educational associations such as the Secondary Heads Association) have formulated a view of the key problems facing England and Wales in this area and have explored ways of changing the current situation. This loose 'alliance' does not share a total consensus over the nature of the problem or the most appropriate solutions but it does hold a view that radical change will have to take place in the very near future and that this is crucial for our economic survival.

The 'alliance' has set an agenda for change which dominates current discussion on 16–19 education and training. The principal concerns are:

- the need to increase participation and attainment rates post-16;
- the need to devise a coherent curriculum and qualification system in which academic and vocational elements are equally valued and carry credit transfer;
- the need to improve the quality of teaching and learning;
- the need to develop coordinated approaches at all levels to the planning and delivery of 16–19 education and training.

In Part 1 of the book Tom Whiteside explores the emergence of this 'alliance' and their agenda for change. This section sets the scene for the contributions in Part 2 which describe and analyse specific vehicles for change. In planning this section a difficult choice had to be made in terms of deciding on an appropriate structure. Rather than attempting to impose an artificial integrated framework which provided an optimistic view of the existing state of coherence, it was decided that the format should reflect the current divisions and tensions in the system. Within the context of the agenda for action, authors, wherever possible, have pointed to the connections between the various vehicles for achieving change. This inevitably leads to a degree of overlap between the different contributions but was felt to be vital for exploring the contributions made by different developments to the agenda for change. Various approaches to bringing about change are examined in detail, grouped under four headings:

Change through certification

This section considers recent developments in academic, vocational and pre-vocational course provision and, in particular, focuses on the key role of changes in the system of qualifications as a vehicle for effecting change.

Change through process

This section is concerned with attempts to bring about significant change in teaching and learning styles and focuses, in particular, on the key role of new approaches to the assessment and recording of achievement and the contribution of core skills to the curriculum of all 16–19 year olds.

Change through funding

During the last decade, the Department of Employment and the Department of Trade and Industry have attempted to influence the nature and rate of change in 16–19 education and training by the use of funding strategies. Two contrasting approaches are examined through a consideration of the use of 'categorical funding' in the Technical and Vocational Education Initiative and the recent delegation of funding for much of vocational education post-16 to the locally controlled Training and Enterprise Councils.

Institutional Change

In this section the impact of this change is considered at the institutional level and issues are explored that need to be addressed if the agenda is to be realized.

In Part 3 Louise Kidd assesses the possibility of significant progress in relation to the agenda for action in the face of competing financial claims and a shifting political agenda.

In the book we attempt to provide a coherent overview of recent significant change in post-16 education and training. The book is aimed at both the student and the practitioner and it is hoped that the issues covered, the detailed bibliography and the glossary will be of particular value to those seeking information in this area.

The contributors to the book have all been working in the area of 16–19 education and training in a variety of roles. A number have been directly involved in the management of the provision at the institutional, area and LEA level. Others have been involved in supporting staff development and in monitoring and evaluation activities in this area. The perspectives adopted by the authors differ according to their varying priorities and backgrounds.

PART 1

Towards a Coherent Policy

CHAPTER 1

The 'Alliance' and the Shaping of the Agenda

Tom Whiteside

During the 1980s a new and powerful consensus on the 'definition of the situation' regarding post-16 education and training emerged, supported by powerful interest groups in both of the major political parties, industry, training and education. Drawing on networks established at first to respond to the dramatic rise in youth unemployment in the 1970s, an 'alliance' across the political spectrum has been formed linked by a commitment to changing fundamentally the nature and extent of post-16 education and training. The main partners in this 'alliance' have changed over time but include, among others, significant groups within each major political party, the Department of Employment (DE), the Department of Trade and Industry (DTI), the Confederation of British Industry (CBI), the Trades Union Congress (TUC) and to varying extents powerful groups of supporters in the different sectors of the educational system.

The themes emphasized by the different parties in the 'alliance' have varied and there has been vigorous debate within it on contested issues. For example, key differences of opinion exist in two central areas. First, there is the issue of whether the system can be changed by continued incremental reform or whether the scale of the problem is such that a root-and-branch redesign is required (these terms are taken from Maclure, 1991a). Second, there is the problem whether the 'market' approach being adopted by the Conservative Government and supported by the CBI will produce the high quality skills needed for the labour force of the future or whether a more planned approach will be necessary. There are indications that in the 1990s the 'alliance' will come under increasing strain as resources become more limited and older agendas relating to youth unemployment re-emerge

The 'alliance' has become much broader in its composition and outlook than those groupings of the early and mid-1980s described by their supporters as the 'new educationalists' (Ranson et al., 1986) and by their critics in a more disparaging way as the 'new vocationalists' (see, for example, Gleeson, 1987; Holt, 1987; Pollard *et al.,* 1988). Analyses of the development of contemporary education policy have identified similar groupings within the Conservative Party as the 'modernisers' (Jones, 1989) and the 'industrial trainers' (Dale, 1983). The party that has been missing in any direct form from the current 'alliance' and these previous groupings has been the Department of Education and Science (DES). Ever since they were directly and deliberately omitted from one of the major educational initiatives of the 1980s, the Technical and Vocational Education Initiative (TVEI), their role in relation to change in this area has been ambiguous and at best can be seen as supportive of the need for incremental change in this field of education.

The origins of the 'alliance'

Lord Young (1990) has written about a significant shift in thinking which took place in the 1970s as industrial and political decision-makers began to challenge the assumption that Britain was inevitably in a long-term decline. The key question became how to arrest the decline and turn Britain once again into a major economic power. The answer that emerged was that Britain must compete in the high technology, high value-added markets. As one industrialist vividly put it 'either we succeed in high-tech, or we become a peasant community' (Institute of Manpower Studies, 1984, p.66).The arguments contained in analyses of the problems of British society such as Barnett's *The Collapse of British Power* (1972) and *The Audit of War* (1986) and Wiener's *English Culture and the Decline of the Industrial Spirit 1850–1980* (1981) contributed to the development of a set of beliefs among politicians and industrialists that one of the central causes of Britain's prolonged economic decline lay in its education and training system.The view emerged that human resources were the major factors in international success and that successful competition with other countries would require the development of skills in the workforce; 'people have become the key to competitiveness' (CBI, 1989, p.16). Support for this view is found in a recent American work on factors affecting the competitive advantage of nations which concluded that 'Britain will not regain innovation-driven status without a world-class educational and training system encompassing all socio-economic and ability levels' (Porter, 1990, p.720). As Sir Christopher Ball has argued 'the quality of the education and training of the workforce is the single most important factor in determining economic competitiveness. By itself it may not be a **sufficient** condition for national economic success, but it is certainly a **necessary** condition' (Ball, 1991a, p.5).

Critical to the emergence of the 'alliance' was the creation of the Manpower Services Commission (MSC) in 1973 which saw itself in the forefront of developing 'a new vision of society and the economy' which would require 'a complete overhaul of Britain's education and training system' (Ainley and Corney, 1990, pp.1 and 2). The scale of the problem facing Britain was recognized from the beginning. In the absence of an established tradition of quality vocational education the issue was how to create a modern and effective training culture which would contribute to a new industrial renaissance. In *A New Training Initiative* (DE, 1981) the MSC stressed the central role of systematic training for all in the process of industrial regeneration and outlined national training objectives for a modern industrial nation. The second of these objectives was that 'we must move towards a position where all young people under the age of 18 have the opportunity, either of continuing in full-time education, or of entering training, or a period of planned work-related training and education' (DE, 1981, p.6). The vehicles for the delivery of these objectives came to be the Youth Training Scheme (YTS) and the Technical and Vocational Education Initiative (TVEI). The pressures of the need to respond to rapidly rising youth unemployment dominated the approaches of the early 1980s but the pressure for change was given added impetus by the influence that Industry Year (1986) had on those involved. There is little doubt that its underlying themes made considerable impact on many of the leading industrial and political decision-makers and that conferences and meetings brought together key individuals from both industry and the different sectors of education who began to share their definitions of problems and potential solutions.

As the rate of unemployment, including that of youth unemployment, began to drop in Britain from 1986 onwards, the main area of debate changed from how to meet the growing social and political problem of youth unemployment to the broader agenda of the New Training Initiative (NTI). How were we to ensure that young people had the skills required to play a part in a rapidly changing society and that people had the opportunities to learn new skills during the course of their working lives? A succession of official reports such as *Employment for the 1990s* (DE, 1988) stressed that the most critical areas of employment growth would occur not in basic manufacturing, but in sectors such as advanced manufacturing, information and high technology and specialized services. Successful businesses would require decentralized management styles, effective use of new technologies and a highly skilled, adaptable and creative working force. It would no longer be appropriate to concentrate on the education of a small leadership élite; the general workforce would need high-level skills and would need to be motivated and capable of learning new skills over their entire working life. In 1981 there were 7 million higher-level jobs, in 1989 8 million and the prediction is that by 2000 there will be slightly fewer than 9.5 million The Government's current plans are based on the 'estimate that over 80 per cent of the new jobs created in the 1990s will come into this broad category' (Jackson, 1991, p.15).

In many ways this type of analysis differs little from the work of the Institute of Manpower Research at Warwick University and that of the Institute of Manpower Studies (Hayes *et al.*, 1982;1983) which in the early 1980s provided similar arguments at the time of the introduction of the YTS. The difference was that the documents now stressed how the emerging skill shortages were likely soon to be exacerbated by the substantial fall in the number of 16–19-year-olds in the population. The scale of the change in the 16–19 age group was particularly stressed with the number of 16-year-olds falling from 889,000 in 1985 to 705,000 in 1995. Between 1987 and 1995 the number of 16–19-year-olds is going to fall by over 850,000 (NEDO, 1988). The 'demographic time bomb', as it was increasingly called, received enormous publicity and after a very effective campaign the DE had to produce a document entitled *Defusing the Demographic Timebomb* (NEDO, 1989) in an attempt to try to reassure employers that there were ways of responding to the problem other than by wage-bidding for young people. It was this demographic pressure which underlined to many in the Government and industry 'the urgency and importance of reforms in Britain's education system...' (DE, 1988, p.18).

The challenge facing Britain continues to be considerable. At the beginning of the 1980s, when the NTI was introduced, the MSC described the British workforce as 'one of the least trained workforces in the industrial world' (MSC, 1982, p.2). By the end of the decade the CBI report (1989, p.16) *Towards a Skills Revolution* was still pointing to repeated studies having shown that 'Britain's workforce is under-educated, under-trained and under-qualified'. In his 1990 Presidential Address to the British Association Sir Claus Moser drew considerable publicity with his call for education to go to 'the top of the national agenda, with the 1990s becoming our Decade for Education' (Moser, 1990, p.6). The Government quickly responded to the move by referring to the 1990s as the 'Skills Decade' while the leadership of the Labour Party refers to education and training as being the 'commanding heights' of the modern economy (see, for example, Labour Party, 1991).

In a similar way education and training post-16 has emerged as a key political issue in most major industrial economies. In Europe, Australasia and the United States this area has been crucial as they have considered how to maintain or restore their international competitiveness particularly as they looked nervously at the emerging strength of the economies of the Pacific Basin. Even in the economic success stories of the Pacific Basin, reform of education and training has become a political priority (Porter, 1990). Guthrie and Pierce have argued that the issue of how to maintain or restore international competitiveness is 'currently the most intense force propelling national policy' (Guthrie and Pierce, 1990, p.180) and have written of the 'globalisation of educational reform'. They argue that the emerging global economy virtually demands that nations address similar educational issues with a resultant increasing international convergence of national educational policies. For students of educational history many of the arguments have a familiar ring. It is interesting to note that the last time such 'convergence' theories, with their functionalist overtones and intellectual support from human capital theory, were in the ascendancy in the early 1960s, proposals were also being advanced for large-scale changes in post-16 education and training. For example, the Robbins Report (Committee on Higher Education, 1963) used arguments for the rapid expansion of higher education that would not have been out of place in any of the reports of the late 1980s and early 1990s.

The agenda for action

The 'alliance' has formulated an 'agenda for action' which has gained wide support and has received national publicity in newspaper campaigns such as The *Independent's* School Charter (June, 1991). The agenda reflects familiar concerns:

- the need to increase participation and attainment rates post-16;
- the need to devise a coherent curriculum and qualification system in which 'academic' and 'vocational' elements are equally valued and carry credit transfer;
- the need to improve the quality of teaching and learning;
- the need to develop coordinated approaches at all levels to the delivery of 16–19 education and training.

The power of the agenda has certainly influenced those in government. Prior to the publication of the 1991 White Paper the Secretary of State pointed out that his joint aims with the Secretary of State for Employment were 'to increase participation, to raise attainment, to provide a clear, recognized system of qualifications, and to enable institutions providing education and training to be more flexible' (Clarke, 1991c, p.2) However, as we shall see, although many elements of the agenda appear to be shared, there are still areas of difference in relation to perceptions of the scale of the problem faced and of what action should be taken to realize these aspirations.

Increasing participation and attainment rates post-16

During the 1980s and the early 1990s reports on both post-compulsory education and higher education (see, for example, CBI, 1989; Royal Society of Arts (RSA), 1991; Smithers and Robinson, 1989; TUC 1989, have conventionally started with chronicling Britain's low levels of participation and attainment in post-16 education. The reports start from a general view of the British system as characterized by early selection and low participation.

Britain, and more particularly England and Wales, has traditionally had a low level of 16-year-olds staying on in full-time education after the minimum leaving age. Throughout the latter part of the 1980s the figure was around 50 per cent with a third of those reaching the end of compulsory schooling having no useful qualifications to show for at least 11 years in full-time education. This resulted in an historically low proportion of 18–21-year-olds entering higher education. The Government has pointed to recent changes such as the introduction of the General Certificate of Secondary Education (GCSE) having led to improvements in all these areas. For example, in 1991 the Secretary of State stated that provisional figures for 1990–91 indicated 60 per cent of 16-year-olds continuing in full-time education and significant increases in the proportion of 18-year-olds entering higher education (1 in 5 of 18–19-year-olds in 1990–91 compared with 1 in 8 ten years before) (Kenneth Clarke, Hansard, 20 May 1991). At the time of writing the explanations for these changes are still not clear. The marked increase in staying-on rates may be linked to increased levels of attainment following the introduction of the GCSE and the creation of new attitudes to staying on, or may be more related to the rapidly changing labour market for young people brought about by the recession.

However these changes are viewed, Britain still has a much lower participation rate than most of our industrial competitors. The roughly 50–60 per cent remaining in post-16 full-time education in 1990–91 compares unfavourably with the USA, Japan and Korea where over 85–90 per cent remain in full-time education. Micklewright *et al.* (1989) have shown in a study of the staying-on rates in European Community countries in 1970/1 and 1983/4 that only Greece had a lower proportion of 16-years-olds in education in 1983/4, and that even here the proportion for boys was higher than that in Britain. Moreover the differences between Britain and the rest of the Community have become more marked over time. In ninth place in both 1970/71 and 1983/4, the United Kingdom experienced an 11 percentage point increase in the proportion of 16-year-olds staying on at school between the two dates compared with a figure of 20 percentage points for the 10 member countries as a whole. These differences in participation rates are, not surprisingly, reflected in differences in the highest levels of qualifications achieved by school leavers in the major industrial economies (see, for example, CBI, 1989, p.18).

Analyses have also pointed out the generally low level of vocational education and training for young people in Britain, with the British workforce having considerably fewer vocational qualifications than that of our major industrial competitors. Prais and his co-workers at the National Institute of Economic and Social Research have undertaken a series of sophisticated studies, attempting to compare Britain's system of education and training with that in other countries, particularly Germany and France. In a pioneering and highly influential paper published in 1981, Prais undertook a comprehensive comparison of the vocational qualifications of the labour force in Britain and Germany. The main finding of the study was that the essential difference between Britain and Germany was not in the proportions of the populations with university degrees (or their equivalents), but in the proportions with intermediate qualifications, such as apprenticeships, City and Guilds or secretarial qualifications. Sixty per cent of the German workforce fell into this category compared with only 30 per cent in Britain. In later work, Prais and Wagner (1983) have claimed that the German schooling system provides a broader curriculum, combined with significantly higher levels of mathematical attainment for a greater proportion of pupils, than does the English system. This study, along with later work examining specific industries, has contributed to the widely held view that the English system of post-16 education and training is too much influenced by the prestigious 'academic' route designed to meet the needs of an academic élite. Work by Steedman (1990) examining the period 1979–88 has shown that Britain's recent policies to improve educational and vocational qualifications have increased the numbers in employment holding lower-level general educational qualifications, but have failed to increase the numbers with intermediate vocational qualifications. She argues that 'the greatest gap is at the lowest level of intermediate qualification (craft or NVQ Level 3) and there is a tendency for higher level skills to be progressively "drawn down" in Britain to plug the gap' (Steedman, 1990, p.56).

The Government has argued, largely on the basis of the development of the YTS, that there has been a substantial increase in the proportion of young people gaining high quality training and higher level qualifications. Critics question whether the YTS is providing high quality training, and whether such training is meeting the long-term needs of young people or employers as a group (Finegold *et al.*, 1990, p.11). The YTS has increased the number of young people attaining 'recognized' vocational qualifications, but these have only been at the lower levels, have been based on short part-time courses and are at levels that would be regarded as pre-vocational in other countries (see, for example, Jarvis and Prais, 1989). Steedman and Wagner (1989, p.52) point out in an examination of clothing manufacture in Britain and Germany that the 'standards to be attained at the end of the second year (of YTS) are below that reached by German trainees in the first half year of their two to three-year training course'. General reviews of YTS in practice have pointed out how YTS is segmented into a range of very unequal training opportunities, which 'select' young people with very different educational qualifications for training of markedly different quality, with significantly different employment prospects (see, for example Lee *et al.*, 1990). In general, YTS has little currency in the external labour market, and critics argue that YTS has in fact worsened the problem of skill shortages because the subsidies have encouraged new and sometimes inexperienced entrepreneurial trainers to dress up and sell low-skill and insecure work as 'training', in a way which confuses and deskills both occupational labels and the trainees themselves. In particular, disadvantaged trainees suffer, coming up against a set of negative experiences during training and becoming even more 'detached' and alienated.

The debate over increasing participation and attainment post-16 was given a significant impetus with the publication in 1989 of the CBI Vocational Education and Training Task Force report, *Towards a Skills Revolution*. The report started from the declaration that the practice of employing 16–18-year-olds without a training which led to nationally recognized qualifications must stop. It laid down a series of 'world class targets' to be achieved which were judged to be the minimum necessary to bridge the youth skills gap. They proposed:

Immediate moves to ensure that by 1995 almost all young people attain NVQ Level II or its academic equivalent.
By the year 2000 half of the age group should attain NVQ Level III or its academic equivalent.
All education and training should be structured and designed to develop self-reliance, flexibility and broad competence as well as specific skills.
By 1995 at least half of the employed workforce should be working

for updated qualifications within the NVQ framework.
By 2000 half of the employed workforce should attain NVQ Level III
or equivalent.

The Government first quickly incorporated the targets into its thinking
but then retreated from them. They were, however, the basis of the targets set by the Labour Party, in their policy documents (see, for example,
Labour Party 1990; 1991). Modifications have been made to these targets in later reports with the recent RSA report (1991) *Learning Pays*
setting the most ambitious targets by expecting all to achieve at least
Level 3 of the NVQ system or its equivalent during the course of their
lives. The targets for post-16 education are linked to targets for higher
education, with the 1991 White Paper setting the target that one in three
young people will enter higher education by the year 2000 (DES/DE,
1991c). Following the White Paper, and as a result of extreme pressure
from the CBI, the Government, supported by a range of agencies and
organizations, committed itself to a set of National Targets broadly
reflecting those previously identified by the CBI (CBI, 1991).

No indications are given as to what proportion of young people will
follow which routes. How many young people, for example, will follow
the 'academic' route and how many will achieve NVQs? How will
young people be motivated to reach these challenging targets? Can they
be achieved without a sacrifice of quality? These questions have set the
scene for the debate on what are the appropriate curricula and qualification structures post-16, what teaching and learning styles will be necessary to support such increased participation and attainment, and how
coherence will be introduced into the system.

A coherent curriculum and qualification system

The failings of the 'divided' system of British 16–19 education and training have long been evident. The main educational reports of the modern
era, from Crowther onwards, have highlighted the damage this division
has caused to both the national and individual interest. At 16, the system
bifurcates, and students follow 'academic' and 'vocational' routes which
are markedly different in content, style of delivery and assessment While
the 'vocational' route has been reformed in the mid-1980s, particularly
by the Business and Technician Education Council (BTEC), with more
emphasis on student-centred approaches, the incorporation of core skills
and the introduction of integrated assignments, the gap has widened with
the Advanced Level curriculum and assessment remaining essentially
unchanged.

There has been recognition in all the major political parties that there is a division in standards and status between 'academic' and 'vocational' qualifications, that this division is harmful, and that it is imperative to remove it. A consensus has arisen that what we require is

> a model of provision where there [are] no dead ends, all routes [can] lead to paid work or to advanced education, where pathways [are] clearly understood, but frequent links and junctions [allow] those who [wish], to change their minds and take a new direction, and where the A-level examination no longer [dominates] the curriculum and public awareness of what [is] worth doing and having (Ball, 1991b, p.21).

The debate has been about how to achieve this and how radical the steps will have to be. Exasperation has risen among many of the partners in the 'alliance' due to the Government's repeated failures to respond to the challenge, the lack of central direction and the limited nature of many of the proposed solutions to the problems.

There is a long history of failed attempts to reform the Advanced Level curriculum. It was the failure of the Government to respond to the recommendations of the Higginson Committee (DES, 1988) that can be seen as a significant watershed. The Committee was given a narrow brief which was to improve or maintain the system without changing the essential character of Advanced Levels. However, they argued that the present system of Advanced Levels was based too much on the needs of the universities, encouraged premature specialization and that the programmes of study were too narrow. It recommended that students should take five 'broader but leaner' Advanced Levels and study more 'balanced' programmes. The Government's response was to accept the Committee's recommendation that the post-16 curriculum needed broadening, while at the same time rejecting the specific suggestion of a change to five 'leaner' Advanced Levels. The Government pressed instead the claims of AS courses as the main way of broadening the curriculum post-16 (Jackson, 1989). This had been their policy since the introduction of AS in 1984 (DES 1984a) and continued to be a key part of their strategy for broadening the curriculum (DES/DE, 1991a, p.20) despite the evidence that the limited number of students undertaking AS see it as primarily complementing or extending their range of Advanced Level subjects. The Government's other response, first made officially by Kenneth Baker in February 1989, was to suggest a series of core skills spanning the 16–19 curriculum which would enhance and align academic and vocational education. These core skills were to be integrated into existing provision rather than 'bolted on'. They were immediately seized on as one means of countering the narrow specific skills associated with some vocational education and as a way of broadening the narrow 'academic' diet of Advanced Levels. Progress on agreeing lists of core skills has been difficult but hope of advances in this area has been raised as a result of the work undertaken by the National Curriculum Council (NCC) (1990a) and the National Council for Vocational Qualifications (NCVQ) (Jessup, 1990).

In the 'vocational' area the recognition that vocational qualifications were under-valued, under-used, confused and confusing led to the setting up of the Review of Vocational Qualifications (RVQ). Its report (MSC/DES, 1986) recommended a new form of qualification to be described as National Vocational Qualifications, a new framework for such qualifications and the setting up of a new body to carry through the proposals – the NCVQ. The Government accepted the Review's proposals in the White Paper *Working Together – Education and Training* (DE/DES, 1986), set up the National Council and later instructed it to have a comprehensive framework of NVQs in place by the end of 1992. The NCVQ's work has come under increasing criticism, particularly that NVQs are too narrow, too concerned with low-level task-based standards (Steedman and Wagner, 1989) and are unlikely to lead to training for tomorrow's competence (Hayes, 1989). Jarvis and Prais' study of training for retailing in France and Britain concluded that the NCVQ's proposed lower levels of qualifications for these trades are

> narrowly job-specific ('competence based'); their exclusion of externally-marked written tests of technical knowledge and of general educational subjects will, we fear, lead to a certificated, semi-literate under-class – a section of the workforce inhibited in job-flexibility, and inhibited in the possibilities of progression (Jarvis and Prais, 1989, p.70).

A more recent attempt by the Government to bring in changes which will 'certainly bridge(s) the divide ' (Kenneth Clarke, Hansard, 20 May 1991 col. 653) are outlined in the White Paper *Education and Training for the 21st Century* (DES/DE, 1991a; 1991b). The proposals aim to 'bridge the divide' by promoting equal esteem for academic and vocational qualifications and clearer and accessible paths between them. The proposals are based on the continuance of Advanced Levels which are described as 'successful and well respected examinations, which are steadily taken by an increasing proportion of pupils' and which the Government commits itself to maintaining and controlling so that their high standard is preserved. The new introductions are Diplomas at Advanced and Ordinary Levels and the development of more General NVQs alongside the more occupationally-specific NVQs already in existence. The precise nature of the Advanced Diploma was to be a matter for consultation but the White Paper saw it as possibly being awarded to 'those gaining two A Levels at grade C or above, an equivalent combination of A and AS, equivalent vocational qualifications, or a combination of A Level, AS and vocational qualifications' (DES/DE, 1991a, p.24). The Consultation Paper on the Advanced and Ordinary Diploma added little to the White Paper except a very clear signal that core skills are not going to be integral to the development of Advanced Levels.

The White Paper's proposals, incrementalist in their approach, kept intact, in the name of quality, the distinctions between the 'academic' and the 'vocational' paths while also trying to ensure 'parity of esteem' by repeating the message that 'it is the level of qualification that matters, not whether it is academic or vocational' (Clarke, 1991c, p.4). The only educational group to applaud openly the White Paper's position was the Head Masters Conference. They were rejected by most of the 'alliance' who, in the light of the golden opportunity presented by demographic changes, favour a more fundamental 'root-and-branch' approach.

In Sir Claus Moser's words,

> The tendency, in a class-divided society, is still to think in terms of reforming academic and vocational streams separately. More sensible, and appropriate to the way knowledge and skills are changing, is to reject this division and to think along the lines of the Baccalaureat or indeed the Abitur, serving the different needs flexibly (Moser, 1990, p.10).

The most influential report outlining a radical approach to the curriculum and qualification structure was the Institute of Public Policy Research report *A British 'Baccalaureat': Ending the Division between Education and Training* (Finegold *et. al.*, 1990). The report should be seen as arising from a background of intellectual debate about whether meaningful distinctions can any longer be made between education and training and between 'academic' and 'vocational' education. Indeed it opens with a quote from Friedrich Ebert, the Founder of the German Social Democratic Party that 'General education is the vocational education of the upper class: vocational education is the general education of the working class' (Finegold *et. al.*, 1990, p.3). It argues that conventional approaches which have focused on the particular weaknesses of the separate 'academic' and 'vocational' streams and sought to reform the divided system rather than to replace it are inappropriate. The early selection – low participation characteristic of the British system is inextricably linked to its divided nature. The abolition of this separation must therefore be the starting point for change.

The report proposes a new unified system of education and training leading to a single 'Advanced Diploma' or 'British Baccalaureat', which it hopes, will encourage the development of a *late selection – high par-*

ticipation system. The Diploma would be modular in structure and would involve an educational core and subject-based options. All students would have to take core modules in the three domains of social and human sciences, natural sciences and technology, and arts, languages and literature and would have to take at least one work/community based module which would involve their using their theoretical studies in a practical context.

The Institute's report influenced a number of key bodies. The Labour Party committed itself to creating a clear unified qualifications structure – the Advanced Certificate for Education and Training (ACET) – to replace the present jungle of qualifications. The qualification structure envisaged would contain modules which would be transferable between institutions, would be offered in both full-time and part-time mode, would be open to entry at any age and completed at the participant's own pace and would comprise both core and optional modules. The Royal Society's 1991 report proposed a similar modular structure which would use credit accumulation and transfer to bridge the divide between the sciences and the arts, as well as between academic and vocational education. A single diploma-based qualification would replace existing qualifications and all students would study three areas: social, economical and industrial; scientific, mathematical and technological; and creative, language and aesthetic, as well as engaging in specialized study. These modular arrangements should ensure that fewer students would leave with no worthwhile qualifications post-16. In a Presidential address to the Institute of Physics Professor Blin-Stoyle pointed out that '25.2 per cent of those on the physics tramline failed the (Advanced Level) examination and had nothing to show for it' (Sanders, 1991).

All models based on a single diploma leave certain key questions unanswered in relation to the creation of a coherent curriculum and qualification structure. Can such a diploma be a uniform 'marketable' award, or will it offer the facade of a single award while masking key differences in real market value? How will the prestige of the vocational routes be raised so that they challenge academic routes in their popularity? Can this be achieved whether or not Advanced Levels remain? Can equivalences be arrived at between academic and vocational qualifications or modules? What will be the significance of differentiating clearly between occupationally-specific and more general NVQs? Have the structures sufficient flexibility and equivalences to offer 'marketable' qualifications at both 17+ and 18+? Will it require a new qualification at 17+? Can modular structures be developed which support coherent learning pathways and do not threaten the 'quality' of existing courses? Do the structures allow for curriculum breadth to be delivered at a level which will ensure quality? Will many of these developments be threatened by changes to pre-16 provision which re-emphasize written assessment as opposed to course-based assessment and external assessment as opposed to internal assessment?

The revolution in learning

There is a consensus that to achieve 'Better motivation: Higher Achievement' (DES/DE, 1991a, p.46) to reach the world class targets, new styles of teaching, learning and assessment will have to be encouraged. While the situation in compulsory schooling has improved from the early 1980s, when HMIs (Welsh Office, 1982) observed that many schools in Wales, particularly in the urban industrial areas, had absence rates in the fourth and fifth years consistently in excess of 25 per cent, there is no doubt that sizeable sections of young people still finish their period of compulsory schooling disaffected and 'bored' with schooling, wishing to leave at the earliest opportunity. Indeed there are anxieties that this proportion may well increase in the future with the introduction of the National Curriculum and the changes to the assessment arrangements for the General Certificate of Secondary Education.

Throughout the 1980s a range of curriculum initiatives, often with the explicit aim of tackling student motivation, have contributed to a re-evaluation of the processes of learning for the 16–19 age group. Starting with pre-vocational programmes such as City and Guilds 365 and the Certificate of Pre-Vocational Education (CPVE) and often supported by funds from the TVEI, a variety of new approaches has been explored. Among the most significant have been:

- the introduction of shorter units of learning with clear assessment criteria;
- recognition of the central role of tutoring and the importance of guidance;
- acknowledging and recording a broader range of student achievements;
- promotion of teaching and learning styles which encourage student autonomy;
- recognition of the need to remove barriers to learning so that students can study at a place, pace and time appropriate to their needs.

However, there is still a 'black box' in most of the reports as to how, without a massive increase in resources, these motivation problems are to be overcome and the world class target figures for participation and attainment are to be achieved. If the 'revolution' which up to now has been concentrated in low-status areas of the curriculum is to be consolidated, the quality of teaching and learning post-16 is going to be one of the most critical areas. The demands of the new approaches are considerable and will represent a challenge, particularly to those working in the 'academic' area whose job satisfaction has largely been gained by teaching their subject to the highest level possible. Indeed HMI reports point out that much of the teaching and lecturing observed will be inappropriate to the needs of the new groups staying on beyond 16. Too many lessons are still characterized by 'a narrow range of teaching methods and approaches, dictated notes, little or no discussion, questions asking mainly for recall of facts and, very often, low expectations of their students' abilities' (HMI, 1989a).

The confusion in the curriculum and qualification system of 16–19 education and training is mirrored in the routes to becoming a teacher. 'Academic' teaching post-16 is usually approached by a Post Graduate Certificate of Education course while 'vocational' teaching is entered either through technical teacher training or by direct entry followed by post-experience training. In the past staff development programmes have tended to be segmented and based on the needs of individual courses. The division in routes has been under strain for some time with increasing numbers of students following 'academic' routes in Colleges of Further Education and Tertiary Colleges and 'vocational' routes being followed in institutions run under school regulations. Key issues arising from the proposed changes are going to be whether a more 'dedicated' post-16 teacher preparation will be necessary and what qualities should be looked for in teachers in this sector in the future.

Flexible Learning has been seen by some members of the 'alliance' as a way of unlocking the 'black box'. It has become the 'best word' of the early 1990s replacing 'enterprise' in its value and appeal. The Employment Department (ED) has vigorously promoted the expansion of Flexible Learning and set a target of embedding student-centred Flexible Learning into the curriculum of all 14–19-year-olds by 1993. Flexible Learning operates as an umbrella term drawing together a wide range of approaches to developing new styles of teaching and learning. Its breadth is affirmed in a book by one of its proponents who argues that Flexible Learning is 'just...good teaching and learning' (Waterhouse, 1990, p.73). Its value is seen as lying in its capacity to generate effective learning, increase motivation and promote achievements. It gives students increasing responsibility for their own learning and development and because of the nature of the learning process enables students to develop core skills and competencies at the same time as acquiring subject-specific knowledge and understanding. In so doing enthusiasts claim that it prepares young people for the style of learning increasingly expected in further and higher education and in employment (DE, 1991, p.4). The emphasis placed on this approach is evident in the 1991 White Paper (DES/DE, 1991a) where increasing use of open and flexible learning 'techniques in which Britain leads the world' is supported to encourage young people to learn at a pace and place that suits them.

Whether these new styles of teaching and learning are appropriate ways of increasing the participation and attainment of social groups who have not traditionally participated in education post-16 must remain an open question. Reducing the dependence of the student on the teacher should be welcomed, but it must be viewed within a framework which sees the crucial role teachers play as significant role models for students from disadvantaged social groups. The danger is that Flexible Learning which could offer significant opportunities will be viewed in a narrow managerial way as a mechanism for expanding participation in the system without increasing resources. If this is the case there is a considerable danger that while participation is increased, a marked improvement in attainment will prove more elusive. A major concern must be that there are few signs that this approach is being adopted in teaching students from the most privileged social groups, with the heads of the major public schools proclaiming with pride their low staff:student ratios.

The search for coherence

Concern has been expressed throughout the 1980s that the permanent conflict and competition at national level between Government departments and between agencies operating at the local level and between individual institutions could mean that there will be little progress in delivering quality post-16 education and training. Members of the 'alliance' have been united by their wish to overcome 'the problem of confused and divided responsibilities...at the centre between the roles of the DES and the DE, and at the local level between the LEAs and the TECs' (Ball, 1991a, p.19). However, more than in the other areas, the proposed solutions differ and reflect markedly different approaches to the problem. For some a market approach, combined with a commitment by Government to offering a coherent vocational and training policy and funding to provide foundation skills for all young people, is the right approach (see, for example, CBI, 1989). For others doubts exist whether a market-oriented approach, in a society where employers and individuals have lacked a pro-training culture, will be sufficient to produce the skills needed for the competitive future. This difference in approach can be clearly seen in relation to the issue of how to bring about the elimination of under-18 employment not involving structured education and training leading to recognized qualifications. The CBI Report (1989) *Towards a Skills Revolution* believed this could be achieved through voluntary means, an approach supported by the Government. Other groups (see, for example, Finegold *et al.,* 1990; Labour Party, 1991) were sceptical of how this could be achieved by voluntary means and have argued for legislation ending employment under the age of 18 without associated education and training.

Many reports have pointed out how we lack at the national level a coherent and comprehensive plan for education, training and employment post-16. The Senior Chief Inspector of Schools pointed out in his Annual Report for 1988–9 that,

> a serious impediment to progress is the absence of general agreement about how this area of education and training should develop and respond to the many pressures for change impinging upon it. ...The risk is that without clear, national guidance it will continue to be hesitant, contradictory, counter-productive, and, above all, slow. There are too many corpses of previous, ill-fated attempts to bring about change littering the 16–19 landscape, for individual interest groups to make the first moves towards unity of purpose and effort. ...National guidance is needed to bring together the interests of education and employment. Without that it is unlikely that change will be effective, or carried out efficiently' (DES, 1990, p.5).

Responsibilities for this sector have been divided between the DES and the DE, with occasional interventions from the DTI. Within each Department there have been further divided groups often advocating plans supporting their interests. Critics have claimed that policy therefore is *ad hoc,* at best incremental and lacking in vision. In the curriculum area the DES has introduced its major initiatives such as the CPVE and AS Examinations while safeguarding the position of the flagship of Advanced Levels. The DE has developed the TVEI, the YTS and the introduction of National Vocational Qualifications. Curriculum approaches developed by one Department such as the TVEI are threatened by developments such as the National Curriculum and City Technology Colleges from another. Inter-institutional collaborative arrangements supported by the TVEI with ED funding have been threatened by DES initiatives such as the Local Management of Schools and Colleges and the possibility of Grant Maintained Status.

The issue of coherence at the national level has for some time been recognized as a key issue. Many reports have called for a Department of Education and Training which would clarify the relationship between education and training by linking the two in a productive way (see, for example, Finegold *et al.,* 1990; RSA, 1991, p.43). These calls are frequently linked with proposals to set up a new over-arching body which could coordinate planning for all kinds of courses and qualifications (see, for example, Finegold *et al.,* 1990; Maclure, 1991b, p.27). Such suggestions are not new. At the height of the power of the MSC, when the unification of education and training was a plank in Labour's programme, Lord Young made an 'unsuccessful bid to succeed Sir Keith Joseph as Minister of Education and Training in a new Department of Enterprise that would fuse together Education and Employment' (Ainley and Corney, 1990, p.97). Others have stressed that what is required is not the setting up of a new Department, because that in itself would not remove the tensions between education and employment, but the recognition of 'disputes...within or between Departments for what they are, and not let them obscure the main task' (Maclure, 1991b, p.28). What all agree is required is the need for commitment from the centre, 'clear sighted, long term, determined leadership, and the assumption of responsibility' (Ball, 1991b, p.19).

The Conservative Government has, however, avoided taking such a leadership role from the centre, perhaps afraid of the financial consequences. It has failed to take a leadership role in producing specific target figures, 'national standards' which can be monitored, and has instead expressed its commitment to the broad aim of increasing participation and attainment rates. This has differed from Labour Party proposals for the introduction of an Education Standards Council which would agree targets for increased participation at 16+ with each Local Education Authority (Labour Party, 1991). The Conservative Government's strategy has been based on the assumption that employers and individuals need to accept a greater share of the responsibility for training and for its costs and has, therefore, devolved 'ownership' of the training and enterprise system to employers. The 1988 White Paper *Employment for the 1990s,* drawing on American experience with Private Industry Councils rather than the German model, signalled the introduction of this more market-led approach to education and training with the setting up at local level of Training and Enterprise Councils (TECs) composed of employers at the top management level drawn from the private sector.

Critics question whether TECs will not be seen as an 'ill-advised, risky and unsuccessful gamble with the future prosperity of Britain' (Coffield, 1990, p.59). The reliance on employers to diagnose and meet skill needs in a cost-effective manner in the national interest is a risk given the lack of evidence that employers in this country are concerned with training. *Competence and Competition* (Institute of Manpower Studies, 1984) showed the greater importance attached to Vocational Education and Training and the higher level of employer support and provision in Japan, the USA and West Germany compared with Britain.

A Challenge to Complacency (Coopers and Lybrand, 1985) pointed out that few employers saw training as central to their business, with training often being viewed as an overhead cost to be reduced in difficult times rather than as an investment. The report *Training in Britain* (DE, 1989) notes some changes in organizational attitudes to training over the 1980s but the evidence is still that it is at the very least questionable whether a sea change in attitudes has taken place among employers. It may be that at the level of the CBI Committees and Conferences such a change in attitudes has taken place but many observers doubt whether this has as yet happened at the local level, in companies of differing sizes and in all industrial sectors. It has been argued that the structure and processes of the British labour market encourage managers to take a short-term view. This means handing control over training to a group who have failed to show, historically and in contemporary contexts, a commitment to training and must therefore raise considerable doubts as to its likely effectiveness. Critics fear that the new arrangements will not result in an appropriate mix of skills for the national economy. Training and Enterprise Councils may be well-equipped to respond to local deficiencies and able to plug gaps but are unlikely to achieve the training effort which will lead to the comprehensive upgrading of skills required for economic survival (Hayes, 1989; Steedman *et al.*, 1991, p.73). They argue that the Government must develop a strategic vision of the capability of the workforce needed to meet international standards and intervene more in the market to ensure that it is in industry's interest to invest in training whatever the current economic conditions. For example, the Vice President of IBM has called for a 'training tax' (Johnson, 1990) and others have called for broader changes to taxation allowances for training. Critics' fears are compounded by the present under-funding of the Training and Enterprise Councils with their energies being currently expended not on determining strategic priorities in training but in finding ways of meeting training guarantees for young unemployed people and the adult jobless. Commentators have pointed out that the system in practice is not a market system for training but an artificial or 'rigged' one (Maclure, 1991b, p.84) or an uneasy 'co-existence of planned provision and the market approach' (RSA, 1991, p.26).

The other key element in the Government's strategy of developing a market in training has been the commitment to extend Training Credits to all 16- and 17-year-olds by 1996 (DES/DE, 1991a). Theoretically this gives power to the consumer, the young person, rather than to the provider and will increase competition in the education system and make institutions more consumer responsive. However the indications are that the importance of credits is seen more at the level of attitude change, 'to bring home to both employers and young people the importance of training' (Clarke, 1991c, p.8) rather than in terms of giving more power to the young person.

A final issue of concern is how rational planning of 16–19 provision is to be achieved in this market-dominated approach. The planning and monitoring functions of the Local Education Authority appear to be in conflict with the market philosophy on which the Training and Enterprise Councils are based. This conflict, along with the increasing diversification of institutions in the post-16 sector, some under Local Authority control and some not, appear to make for limited attempts at planning and rationalization. Proponents of the market model argue that the waste that follows from competitive duplication will be more than compensated for by the increased efficiency brought by competitive enterprise.

Broader issues

The main elements in the agenda of the 'alliance' were formed in the latter stages of the 1980s as the country moved into a period of economic recovery. Its rhetoric of increasing the supply of educated labour to meet the demands of a changing economy within a broader framework of increasing international competition faced little challenge. From the vantage point of the harsher economic realities of the early 1990s some broader issues in relation to the agenda of the 'alliance' can be explored.

In general the rhetoric of the 'alliance' has as yet gone politically unchallenged and unexamined. The breadth of the 'alliance', the involvement of free-market politicians and the legitimacy obtained from substantial industrial involvement have led to most of the right-wing Conservative think tanks avoiding direct confrontation with the proposals and the policies of the 'alliance'. Although some have claimed that the 'alliance' lost political ground in the late 1980s (see, for example, Chitty, 1991), in general Conservative educationalists have given little attention to the question of the relationships between education and the economy. Sheltering under an insistence either on the market or quality, the market right have failed to explain how the market would ensure an appropriately educated workforce for the increasingly competitive future, while the paternalist right in their insistence on quality have failed to address the issue of how the population should be schooled for a rapidly changing future. This has meant that as long as modernization and its outcomes could be interpreted as extending the diversity in schools and colleges and as part of a larger agenda of improving standards the 'alliance' has not faced criticism (Knight, 1990). Politically however, for supporters of the 'alliance' within Government, this has involved not challenging traditional safeguards of quality such as Advanced Levels.

Doubts must remain whether the proposed agenda for change will not be resisted strongly by Conservative educationalists. Flexible learning, student-centred learning, accreditation of prior learning, modular routes, credit accumulation and transfer – key strategies for the 'alliance' – seem to be directly in conflict with the views of Conservative educationalists who have already opposed moves to child-centred teaching and have argued forcefully for the virtues of didactic teaching. The moves to higher participation rates coupled with dramatic increases in attainment rates and the consequent pressure to change or dilute the 'gold standard' attached to Advanced Levels make conflict appear certain. There has already been some conflict centred round institutional structures; there would seem to be ample scope for more in relation to the content, processes and appropriate assessment strategies in post-16 education and training.

Lessons from across the water

At a time when 'parity of esteem' is being advocated as the way to 'bridging the divide' it is worthwhile examining the French experience as they have moved towards the commitment given in the 1989 *loi d'orientation* that the system would by the year 2000 have 80 per cent of the age group achieving the *Baccalaureat*. To achieve this, while at the same time maintaining or increasing educational standards, the French government has supported the development of the *Baccalaureat professionel*, a broadly based course including work experience. There has been a rapid increase in the proportion of the age group obtaining the *Baccalaureat*, from 24.2 per cent in 1975 to 47.9 per cent in 1990. Fears have been expressed that this expansion is being achieved at the expense of a fall in standards. The *Baccalaureat* has come under ever-increasing scrutiny which included the socialist Prime Minister, Edith Cresson, asking whether students need to continue their general education until the age of 16, and whether apprenticeships would not provide better vocational opportunities than the *Baccalaureat* for those less suited to academic work. Such remarks should be seen as arising within a similar economic climate to our own and as related to the emergence of political unrest among young people during the early part of 1991.

Among the educational issues giving rise to these questions have been the continuing dominance of the 'academic *Baccalaureat*' which is reflected in student choices, the increasing numbers completing the *Baccalaureat* who wish to go on to higher education, the lack of adjustment of the labour market to *Baccalaureat* holders at 18, the high proportion of students (20 per cent)who repeat the first year of their

Baccalaureat course (Bert, 1988, in Lewis, 1989, p.375), the relatively low proportion (50 per cent) who finish in three years (Ruffieux, 1988, in Lewis, 1989, p.375) and the difficulties pupils who obtain the *Baccalaureat professionel* have in coping with the transition to higher education courses. Additionally, the rapid expansion of young people undertaking higher level qualifications has led to an imbalance whereby youngsters studying for the *Baccalaureat* have failed to find the type of employment they hoped for and have increasingly taken jobs that might otherwise have been available to those with basic vocational qualifications (Jarvis and Prais, 1989).

Education and employment

Social scientists have raised broader political questions about the effects of the single-minded focus on improvements in education and training. In this they have been influenced by the work of French social scientists (see, for example, Maurice *et al.*, 1986) who have argued that distinctive national structures of educational provision, methods of work organization and the style and institutional arrangements of industrial relations combine to influence the ways in which skills are defined and provided for, and that the conjunctions of these factors vary dramatically from country to country. Drawing on this approach, Finegold and Soskice (1988) argue that Britain is locked into a 'low-quality/low skill equilibrium' in which the majority of enterprises are staffed by poorly trained managers and workers who produce low-quality goods and services. The term 'equilibrium' is used to describe a self-reinforcing network of societal and state institutions which interact to stifle the demand for improvements in skill levels. To break into this by focusing on one variable, they argue, is likely to lead to limited results. Better education and training post-16 may be necessary for economic success but it may not be sufficient without the accompanying reform of other institutions.

If change is to occur significant shifts will have to take place in the structure and processes of the labour market. Britain has traditionally been characterized not only by its low rates of post-compulsory education but also by its high rates of early entry into the labour market (Ashton and Lowe, 1991). Under the influence of youth unemployment, the labour market for young people changed dramatically during the 1980s with fewer young people moving directly from school into a full-time job. For most young people the transition from school to work is now an 'interrupted' or 'staged' one (Roberts *et al.*, 1986). However, there were clear signs that in the period of economic recovery towards the end of the 1980s increasing proportions of young people were once again entering work directly at 16. Young people in Britain still have a deep-rooted commitment to getting paid employment at the earliest possible opportunity. Bynner has pointed out how 'getting a job is still central to adult identity for...boys and girls, and especially amongst those who have the least prospect of getting one – the low attainment group' (Bynner, 1991, p.193). The extent of the change necessary should not be underestimated. It requires a change in cultural values so that it is assumed 'it is worthwhile for everyone to be well educated and trained' (Baker, 1989). This will involve changes in employer attitudes to the use of young people in the work place, changes in employers' recruitment and reward policies, and change in young people's approaches to continuing education and training.

Improving access, participation and even attainment post-16 is unlikely to be achieved unless young people perceive 'staying on' as giving them access to the occupations or destinations to which they aspire. Previous attempts to reform the nature of 16–19 education and training have foundered on the lack of suitable routes for youngsters who stayed on in education until the age of 18. This has been particularly the case with young people who have followed the 'vocational' route. Indeed, entering post-16 education may mean that routes are closed to the young person, e.g., apprenticeship and training schemes, while other studies have indicated that 'failure' post-16 may mean that young people substantially harm their employment prospects by staying on (Raffe, 1984). If the current attempts at reform are to be successful it will require a change in the long-standing preference of employers for recruiting at 16 and for pulling many relatively well-qualified students out of the education system at this stage.

The agenda of the 'alliance' is going to be difficult to sustain in the 1990s. There is a considerable danger that short-term concern with the rising numbers of unemployed young people will again dominate the agenda. Markets for educated labour are notoriously susceptible to fluctuations in economic conditions. In 1982 there was a 20 per cent unemployment rate for new university and polytechnic graduates which fell to 8 per cent by 1988 (HMSO, 1990, p.17). The signs are that it is rapidly rising again in the early 1990s. There are also indications of major changes in the employment prospects for young non-graduate labour. In these fluctuating circumstances it is going to be even more difficult to effect the change in societal attitude that is required.

Conclusion

In the remaining sections of this book the areas considered in this chapter are examined in more detail. Each chapter must be viewed in terms of the broader problem of how to achieve the rapid progress in 16–19 edu-

26

cation and training that will be required if Britain is to be 'recast' as a modern industrial nation with a workforce capable of competing in the high value-added markets. The approach that has been adopted builds on the status quo by making gradual incremental changes. That is the approach reflected in the structure of this book, whereas the strategic alternative involves fundamental restructuring of systems of post-compulsory education and training. As the Royal Society of Arts (1991, p.37) has presented it,

> the dilemma for society is acute, since the first approach is acceptable to most interested parties but unlikely to achieve the objectives required; the second, which is probably necessary if we seriously hope to create a learning society, goes against the grain of a traditionally conservative nation.

PART 2

Vehicles for Change

Change through Certification

CHAPTER 2

The Reform of Vocational Education

Alan Sutton

Introduction

In contrast to the 'academic' curriculum, where the Government has
been swift to counter any suggestion of change in the character of provision which would threaten the 'gold standard' of Advanced Levels,
vocational education is currently undergoing fundamental change.
Following the evolutionary developments in vocational education in the
1960s and 1970s, which were essentially concerned with the rationalization of courses, an attempt is now being made to transform radically the
nature of traditional vocational qualifications and their relationship to
each other. The intention is to bring about a major restructuring of the
entire system of vocational education from basic education and training
to the highest professional levels and to put in place nationally recognized qualifications in which outcomes are based on standards of competence which will either be occupation-specific National Vocational
Qualifications (NVQs) or a more broadly based preparation for employment in the form of General National Vocational Qualifications
(GNVQs).

These changes are a response to long-standing perceived deficiencies
in the system of vocational education and training which have been articulated in a series of Government White Papers throughout the 1980s – *A
New Training Initiative* (DE, 1981), *Training for Jobs* (DE, 1984),
Education and Training for Young People (DES/DE, 1985), *Working
Together – Education and Training* (DE/DES, 1986), *Employment for the
1990s* (DE, 1988) and finally *Education and Training for the 21st
Century* (DES/DE, 1991a). Running through these White Papers has
been the identification of the characteristics necessary for any new vocational qualification system: standardization; rationalization; cost-effectiveness; accessibility; equity; clarity and simplicity; opportunities for
continuity, progression and transfer; relevance; comprehensiveness; and
articulation with academic programmes.

The focus on a review of vocational qualifications is part of a broader reform movement to make vocational education and training more responsive to the needs of industry and more client-centred. The first development dating from the White Paper *Training for Jobs* (DE, 1984) was the requirement that FE colleges demonstrate increased responsiveness to the needs of the local labour market when planning course provision. Indeed, a condition of Training Agency funding for Non-Advanced Further Education (later Work-Related FE) which had been transferred from LEAs, was that colleges draw up development plans which demonstrated a recognition of labour market trends. The second development was a move to make the delivery of vocational education more flexible to accommodate clients' needs. This included support for open and flexible learning, an extension of the FE college year and roll-on/roll-off provision. The final development, announced in the 1988 White Paper (DE, 1988), was the shift in the responsibility for the funding and planning of vocational education to employers at a local level with the setting up of Training and Enterprise Councils (TECs). This development will have major implications for 16–19 education and training as TECs now have responsibility for Youth Training, Work-Related Further Education (WRFE), and Education-Business Partnerships.

The background to the current changes

During the 1960s and the 1970s there had been some significant changes in the pattern of vocational courses and qualifications. One such development arose from the Haslegrave Report (DES, 1969) which reviewed the provision for technicians, pointed out the deficiencies and recommended new national arrangements for the administration of a unified pattern of courses for technicians and business and office studies. Subsequently, the Technician Education Council (TEC) was set up in 1973 and created a unitary system with four qualifications. Further rationalization was achieved by the Business Education Council (BEC), set up in 1974, which replaced existing awards with its own three levels: General, National and Higher National Diploma and Certificate. The two organizations merged in 1983 to form the Business and Technician Education Council (BTEC).

Despite these previous attempts at reform, the system of vocational qualifications was still perceived as a barrier to continuity and progression for students. Frequent references to the jungle of qualifications post-16 applied particularly to vocational education and contrasted unfavourably with the more easily understood academic route. Some efforts were made to assist students to identify routes through the system. However, the pattern of provision still remained confusing to many students, parents and employers. Beryl Pratley commented that 'looking back from the position in which we now find ourselves (May 1985), the map of 1980 seems...a model of simplicity compared with the tangle of paths now provided by competing planning authorities' (FEU, 1985).

The need to develop common agreed national standards was the first priority to be identified for the reform of Vocational Education and Training (VET). The intention to move towards national standards was first articulated in objective 1 of *A New Training Initiative* (NTI) (DE, 1981) which called for the reform of an outdated apprenticeship system. It is interesting that NTI did not mention at this stage the term 'competence' as such. It did, however, call for the achievement by 1985 of recognized standards for all the main craft, technician and professional skills to replace time-serving and age-restricted apprenticeships.

The creation of the National Council for Vocational Qualifications

The relative lack of progress in this respect led to the 1985 White Paper *Education and Training for Young People* (DES/DE, 1985) proposing the setting up of a review group with the task of recommending a structure of vocational qualifications which would be relevant to the needs of people with a wide range of abilities. The review group looked at the existing provision and recognized its strengths but also acknowledged its weaknesses: the very large number of qualifications, the overlap and duplication between them, the absence of any clear equivalence of standards, the bias in the assessment methods towards the testing of knowledge rather than skill or competence, and the absence of vocational qualifications in sectors at some levels. The final report (MSC/DES, 1986) called for a National Council for Vocational Qualifications (NCVQ) to rationalize and extend vocational qualifications and to ensure that the qualifications were relevant to employment needs. It recommended a new national framework which should be comprehensible, relevant, credible, accessible and cost-effective.

The recommendations of the 1986 Review of Vocational Qualifications were fully endorsed by the Government in the White Paper *Working Together – Education and Training* (DE/DES, 1986) and the NCVQ was charged with putting the reforms into place by the early 1990s. The Government's remit to NCVQ was to: secure standards of occupational competence and to ensure that vocational qualifications are based on them; obtain comprehensive coverage of all occupational sectors; design and implement a new national framework for vocational qualifications; approve award-bearing bodies; promote vocational qualifications and to establish links with the academic route. NCVQ has played a key coordinating role working with members of the 'alliance' to effect change, with the Training Agency to identify criteria for competence-based assessment, with Lead Industry Bodies (LIBs) and Professional Associations to agree on nationally acceptable standards of competence, with Examination and Validating bodies to accredit qualifications which meet NCVQ criteria, with NCC and SEAC on core skills and finally with NCC, SEAC, CBI, TUC and vocational examination boards on criteria and models for GNVQs.

The aim is to bring all vocational qualifications into a single national system in order to make them more comprehensive and to aid continuity by clearly showing the routes available to those seeking qualifications. The intention is that new NVQs will be allocated to one of five levels across the eleven MSC occupational categories. The NVQ levels of competence are (1) basic or foundation (2) regular (3) skilled (4) advanced and (5) professional. At the higher levels of the NVQ framework, the competence requirements become more demanding and the nature of competence changes to include higher-level skills such as the ability to transfer competence from one context to another and to supervise others.

More recently, NCVQ has been required to establish linkages between the vocational and academic routes and both sets of qualifications have been aligned at the five levels in the NVQ framework. Establishing the equivalence of qualifications was necessary in order to set national standards for attainment spanning the divide, to assist in establishing parity of esteem between the two routes and to facilitate credit transfer. The latest addition to the NVQ framework announced in the 1991 White Paper (DES/DE, 1991a) will be GNVQs, a new third route into employment and higher education discussed in detail in Chapter 4.

The change in the nature of vocational qualifications

The move towards the development of occupational competence based on agreed standards was assisted by the report of the Review of Vocational Qualifications (RVQ) which provided an important definition of a national vocational qualification as 'a statement of competence clearly relevant for work and intended to facilitate entry into or progression in employment, further education and training issued by a recognized body to an individual'(MSC/DES 1986). The document required that this statement of competence should incorporate the assessment of skills to specified standards, relevant knowledge and understanding and the ability to use skills and apply knowledge and understanding to the performance of relevant tasks.

The White Paper (DE/DES, 1986) required the Training Agency to accelerate the process of encouraging representative bodies in all sectors to develop occupational standards of competence. These Lead Industry

Bodies (there are about 150), consisting of representatives of employers and professional associations, were required to develop a map of standards and specifications for their employment sector, to set broadly-based standards of competence and qualifications for each area and level and to work with awarding bodies to devise and reform qualifications. In identifying these standards, LIBs were obliged to take note of design criteria devised by the TA. Initially, when the context of defining standards was the YTS, the focus was on the use of task analysis. However, concern about the narrowness of the standards being set resulted in a decision by the TA and NCVQ that functional analysis should be the basis of the standard setting. This approach breaks down the work role of a particular occupational area into purposes and functions. In the identification of standards, LIBs were starting from different positions. Some had well-developed systems of training and certification but differed in the degree to which they met competence-based criteria, while others already had industrially-based qualifications and national standards.

The NVQs differ from traditional vocational qualifications in their design, accessibility and arrangements for assessment. NVQs consist of five to twenty units of varying size but with a standardized and clear format. Each unit covers a specific role within an occupational area and consists of elements and performance criteria which are the standards which the individual must demonstrate to be deemed competent. Range statements describe the context which the elements of competence cover and provide guidance on the knowledge and understanding required to certificate competence. A criticism of traditional qualifications was the difficulty of gaining access to them for some students. NVQs, by contrast, open up access in that they can be awarded to individuals who meet the required standard irrespective of the time taken or the mode of learning. It is also intended that there should be open access to assessment, either in the workplace or a simulated working environment. Accessibility is also aided by the absence of pre-entry requirements.

The NCVQ credit accumulation and transfer scheme is an important aid to progression and transfer. Credit may be awarded for each unit separately and units may be accumulated for the award of a full NVQ. This allows clients to acquire NVQs unit-by-unit and record their progression in the National Record of Vocational Achievement (NROVA) which was first used in September 1988 and modified in 1990. Secondly, because NVQs awarded by all awarding bodies in an area of competence are based on the same statement of competence, the awards and the constituent units are interchangeable. The credit accumulation and transfer system was introduced in 1988 and is supported by 15 of the major awarding bodies. Credit accumulation and transfer is also aided by the setting up of the national database of vocational qualifications which provide detailed information on NVQs.

In the early stages of the development of standards and accreditation, the Youth Training Scheme (YTS) was the main focus for new standards and qualifications which became the basis for NVQs at Levels 1 and 2. In the majority of cases, standards were set and NVQs accredited at those levels. Progress was not even and an FEU survey in 1989 on NVQs showed that in some occupational areas new standard work had only just started (FEU, 1989a). NCVQ by necessity made use of conditional accreditation recognizing existing vocational qualifications which met certain prerequisities on condition that the awarding bodies entered into a formal contract with NCVQ to reform qualifications based on lead body standards when they became available. However, there has been some concern about the quality of qualifications on offer and about evidence of existing qualifications and skill tests being expediently yoked together and being deemed to satisfy NCVQ criteria, even when they do not (Boffy, 1990b). The pace of accreditation by NCVQ has steadily increased but the original intention of putting the first four levels in place by 1991 has not been met. By 1991 about 250 NVQs had been accredited representing 50 per cent of occupational areas. The Government forced the pace in the 1991 White Paper which set a target coverage of 80 per cent of the occupational areas by 1992 (DES/DE, 1991a). This prompted some concern about the pace of change with questions being asked about whether such a target could or should be achieved.

In the reform movement, the identification of standards of competence has been difficult and protracted not least at the higher levels in the NVQ framework. There has also been tension over the interpretation of competence. The FEU has consistently advocated a broad definition of competence which covers knowledge, understanding, skills, attitudes and a range of experiences as preparation for a variety of adult roles. For their part, NCVQ has reiterated its support for a view of competence which encompasses the abilities to transfer knowledge and skills to new situations, to plan and organize work, to cope with unforeseen situations and to work effectively alongside others. This broader definition of competence contrasts sharply with narrower interpretations adopted by some Lead Industrial Bodies. Some have warned that they have, in too many cases, tended to focus on narrow, mechanistic, easily measurable competencies.

The increasing emphasis on the vocational route

The Government has declared its intention of placing increasing emphasis on the hitherto undervalued and misunderstood vocational route in its bid to increase participation and attainment rates. This could be related to the DES view that there is little hope of achieving the CBI's ambitious targets via the academic route alone, given its determination to preserve the character of A Level provision and to maintain standards. Increased Government attention to the FE sector, previously somewhat of a 'Cinderella', can be traced back to Kenneth Baker's speech to the Association of Colleges for Further and Higher Education in February 1989 (Baker, 1989). More recently, in a speech to the annual conference of the Secondary Heads Association, Kenneth Clarke advised delegates that 'many of (their) students at 16 are better advised to transfer to FE than to stay on in schools' (Clarke, 1991a). Furthermore, Government legislation for April 1993 will put FE and sixth-form colleges centre stage in the challenge to increase post-16 participation rates and attainment levels still further. To cope with the challenge, the Government has promoted a range of strategies. These are to reform the system of vocational qualifications and to promote linkages with the academic route; to improve the rigour of vocational qualifications and to establish parity of esteem between the academic and vocational routes; to encourage more schools to offer vocational courses, and to make available combinations of academic and vocational courses.

According to the recent GNVQ consultation document, the primary aims of the VET system are 'to create an easily understood and universally recognized set of qualifications...and to provide maximum flexibility for students to be able to choose what they want to learn' (NCVQ, 1991). The potential of the new framework and the design specifications of the NVQs to achieve these aims in the longer term are apparent. Within the vocational route there will be clearer tracks for vertical and lateral progression both within and across occupational sectors. It may be, however, that the shift in the nature of qualifications which is being promoted will need a longer time scale than is currently being envisaged. The new infrastructure, arrangements for credit accumulation and transfer, if supported by improved guidance, Individual Action Plans and Records of Achievement, could be a contributory factor in increasing participation rates.

There remains, however, considerable work to translate this vision into reality and the current map of 14–19 routes and qualifications still looks bewildering in the extreme. The changes which have been announced add to the complexity of provision. They include the new Diploma of Vocational Education which will provide a 14–19 vocational route with qualifications at three levels, new overarching national diplomas at Levels 2 and 3 and the introduction of GNVQs.

At the crucial NVQ Level 3, recruitment on to the A Level route continues to be very buoyant despite the steadily increasing numbers of BTEC students. DES statistics suggest that 30 per cent of the 16–19 cohort are following A/AS courses compared with 9 per cent on BTEC. As the 1991 White Paper acknowledges, many aspiring GCSE students are unaware of the vocational alternative to the academic route (DES/DE, 1991a). BTEC is attempting to promote BTEC First and National courses in schools post-16. The number of secondary schools offering BTEC National has increased but it is still an insignificant figure. Given the rigorous BTEC submission requirements for recent industrial experience of staff, time for team meetings and the availability of equipment as well as the cost of accreditation, this is hardly surprising. There will be many commentators who will feel that BTEC courses, including the new GNVQs, are best left to the FE sector.

The take-up of BTEC First qualifications in schools appears to be more significant. There appears to have been a grass-roots demand for this type of qualification to be made available in schools which has led to a relaxation of regulations to allow BTEC First in schools. One hundred and forty schools were offering BTEC First from September 1991 and a further 800 hope to offer the qualification from 1992. This increase is likely to be at the expense of CPVE which has lacked currency value with employers and has had problems in relation to progression on to higher level courses. In contrast, BTEC offers the possibility of clear progression routes. The new Diploma of Vocational Education, which is being piloted by City and Guilds in about 200 schools, is intended to improve possibilities for progression as the new qualifications are planned to span the 16+ divide. It may be that the establishment of the clear vocational route alongside GCSE, as well as the development of vocationally-oriented GCSEs, will be incentives for more young people to continue on the vocational route post-16. The possibility of combining academic and vocational qualifications will be difficult for many schools with small sixth forms. Resource constraints and staffing will force them into making difficult decisions between the separate routes rather than offering provision that spans the divide.

Finally, there are considerable challenges to be faced in the drive to increase participation rates into higher education via the vocational route. The academic route is still the normal one into higher education despite the increased success of students gaining access to polytechnics from the BTEC route. At the present time, approximately 70 per cent of students who enter higher education use A Levels as their main entry qualification. For those who succeed in gaining entry, evidence suggests that those with BTEC perform less well than those students entering with academic qualifications (Smithers, 1991).

A coherent curriculum and qualifications system

There have traditionally been two main tracks in the UK education system post-16. The extent and nature of this academic/vocational divide has, if anything, widened in the 1980s, creating problems for members of the 'alliance' who have sought to close the divide. By the early 1980s, vocational courses were already markedly different from their academic counterparts, in their purpose, structure, arrangements for teaching and assessment and in links with local industry. Further changes resulted from policy statements of examination boards such as BTEC in their publication *Policies and Priorities into the 1990s* (BTEC, 1984). This added the requirement for colleges to introduce more active learning approaches, to devise programmes of integrated assignments, to use real work contexts and to assess, record and report on core skills. By the mid 1980s, differences were very pronounced, particularly as, with the exception of a significant minority of innovative syllabuses and some TVEI promoted modular schemes, A Levels and A Level teaching were largely unchanged. The influence of the changes in vocational qualifications has been to widen the divide still further as more emphasis has been placed on employer-generated occupational competence, assessed where possible in the work place or at least in a realistic simulated working environment.

Recently, pressure from the 'alliance' has built up to close the divide. In the foreseeable future, the most likely scenario will be the maintenance of the separate routes with a third middle route, GNVQs, providing a broadening dimension to the vocational route. Those proposals which advocate eliminating the divide by a complete restructuring on modular lines are, in any case, in a very embryonic form. The more conservative proposals retain the separate routes but establish linkages between them. These invariably require the modularization of A/AS courses to bring delivery structures in line with the vocational route. The major pressure for change is the need to make it easier for students to move between the two routes and to be given credit for interim achievement. A second pressure is the need to vocationalize and broaden the Advanced Level curriculum by the incorporation of core skills; a third is NCVQ's intention to use core skills to improve the status and acceptability of the vocational route for progression to higher education.

Strategies for student movement across the divide have depended on establishing a degree of commonality, dual accreditation and transfer of credit between the two systems. There are examples of attempting to use BTEC National, together with modular A Levels in business studies and science, but experience suggests that the movement of students is one way, from the academic to the vocational. The future of core skills in the Advanced Level curriculum looks set to be a much paler version than that envisaged by NCC despite the fact that NCVQ and NCC are in agreement on the same core skills to be included in vocational and academic qualifications (see Chapter 7).

The revolution in learning

Through the second half of the 1980s, active, student-centred approaches to learning were promoted by the TA, FEU and vocational examination boards Modularization became a significant aspect of course design in pre-vocational and vocational courses, including CPVE and BTEC. Moreover, in response to the demands of TEED for TVEI Extension, attempts have been made by LEAs to produce statements of entitlement for all students in the 16–19 age range. These statements have included an identification of planning principles, the differing contexts and processes of learning, core skills and common learning outcomes. TVEI has been an important influence on developments post-16, challenging schools and colleges to consider the curriculum as a whole rather than as a set of individual courses. It has built on the gains of pre-vocational and vocational courses which have emphasized student-centred approaches to learning. By the time of the Education Reform Act (ERA) in 1988, there was an emerging consensus in the 'alliance' on the main processes of learning underpinning pre-vocational and vocational courses; induction and initial assessment; activity-based and open-learning opportunities; negotiation of learning programmes and targets; planned work or community experience; formative assessment and review; and continuing guidance and personal support.

There is no doubt that the reform of vocational qualifications will have far-reaching implications for further education, the traditional provider of vocational education and training for the design, delivery and assessment of provision. Jessup (1991) claims there is an emerging model of education and training 16–19 which aims to individualize learning and maximize personal achievement and in which guidance and formative assessment are integral parts of learning. This model is assisted by changes to vocational qualifications which make explicit the outcomes of vocational education and training based on criterion-referenced standards of competence. The separation of assessment from delivery in the new NVQs will also mean that FE will lose its monopoly over the award of vocational qualifications.

For some members of the 'alliance', the clear specification of the outcomes of vocational education in standardized units, the possibility of credit accumulation and transfer, and the availability of an NVQ database provide the potential for a learner-centred model of education and training. A change in the culture of colleges resulting in a shift of focus from courses to individual learners is seen as essential if participation and attainment levels are to be increased. The new computerized database will provide a quality of information which has not previously been available on the relationship between occupations and qualifications, and this process will be further enhanced when the database is linked to the Training and Access Points which provide information on education and training opportunities. The availability of clearly defined outcomes will also assist in the accreditation of prior learning and student Action Planning which will form an essential part of the National Record of Achievement. There will need to be provision of a variety of forms of learning to suit individual needs, including Open Learning Workshops and there are proposals to design a national system of open learning and support materials targetted on NVQ units.

The changes also assume that companies and other employer organizations will become major providers of learning opportunities and assessment. To facilitate this, consortium arrangements will need to be established between companies and local providers of education and training. The intended shift in the emphasis to work-based assessment will be very demanding. Colleges will also need to develop strategies for providing assessment on demand on an open-access basis, at the request of the client and making arrangements for the coordination and recording of the continuous record of the individual student's performance. There are clear implications for staff development and for organizational structures and there are suggestions that the potential of the changes will not be realized unless there is an overall organizational response. Some supporters of the 'alliance' have added notes of caution, pointing out the disjunction between rhetoric and reality and warning against accepting too readily the extent of the change already achieved (Shackleton, 1988)

Coherence in policy-making

At the end of the 1980s, a decade of intense activity in which the 'alliance' challenged the entrenched arrangements and attempted to bring greater coherence to courses and qualifications post-16, the system remained set for continuing its essentially separate development. At the national level, the DES re-asserted its dominance as the TA/TEED progressively declined in influence. TVEI found it difficult to challenge the 'gold standard' with its entitlement curriculum. It is noteworthy that there was no mention of core skills and entitlement in the DES/DE White Paper (DES/DE, 1991a). In addition, the divide at 16+ was firmly re-established by the DES with its arrangements for a National

Curriculum 5–16. There appears to be a possibility that TVEI, with its philosophy of developing 14–19 programmes based on principles of continuity and progression, will be regarded by future historians as merely a brief interlude.

Some LEAs, charged under ERA with responsibility for the strategic planning, monitoring and evaluation of provision, have sought to devise coherent development plans for 16–19 which integrate the external demands on the system with initiatives such as YT, WRFE, TVEI, Compacts and RVQ. This task has been difficult even though the majority of these initiatives originated from the Training Agency. Despite these efforts, the school/FE divide remains strong, with FE focusing on coming to terms with WRFE and the implications of NVQs at a time when, for the majority of schools, the National Curriculum and TVEI are still the major priority.

At the local level, a positive feature of TVEI in some LEAs has been the collaborative arrangements for the planning and delivery of modular link courses certificated by Foundation Programmes, CPVE and GCSE. Where these are well organized they can contribute to increased take-up on vocational courses post-16. The effect of LMS on these arrangements is unclear. However, the move to establish BTEC provision in schools, sometimes at the expense of FE, is a reflection of the increased determination in schools as well as FE to increase participation rates to take advantage of the generous 16+ age-weighting factor in formula funding. This competition may threaten collaborative arrangements which will continue to be necessary to provide the combination of courses across the academic/vocational divide anticipated in the 1991 White Paper.

Conclusion

In this chapter, the attempts over the 1980s to reform vocational education have been examined. Mainly they have been directed towards putting in place an infrastructure for the education and training of the workforce as a whole, not just the 16–19 age group. Routes continue to be confused and the future looks potentially more confusing as access to particular routes is no longer the monopoly of particular educational institutions and a 'third route' through GNVQs emerges. The FE and Tertiary Colleges, along with the 'liberated' sixth-form Colleges and the newly 'enfranchised' schools, will all be involved in providing vocational education and training. However, under the pressure of Local Financial Management and increased competition, it looks likely that many institutions will continue to limit their provision to their traditional offerings.

The arrival of the Training and Enterprise Councils and the intended extension of the Training Credits scheme may do little to make planning at the national and local level any more coherent. In the long run the local market solution to the problems of vocational education appears no more capable than its predecessors of challenging the deep-seated and persistent cultural attitudes associated with the low status of vocational education in our society.

CHAPTER 3

The Academic Curriculum - Reform Resisted

David Kerr

The structure of the academic curriculum has remained largely unchanged throughout the 1970s and 1980s, with A Levels surviving as the 'gold standard', despite the efforts of the 'alliance' to reform post-16 education and training. The lack of reform in the academic curriculum post-16 stands in marked contrast to the significant changes introduced into the school curriculum pre-16 and the vocational curriculum post-16. It would be wrong to assume from this lack of change that the academic curriculum has been unchallenged. The introduction of A Levels in 1951 brought in a system which had no insistence on particular subjects, with the choice of subjects being as free as school timetabling and university requirements allowed. There has been debate about whether this was an appropriate curriculum.

Critics have continually used international comparisons to suggest that the excessive concentration on a limited number of subjects, characteristic of the English system, is a weakness rather than a strength. Specialization in the French baccalaureat is a matter of emphasis within a wide course, so that even within the last year at school a mathematics student studies philosophy, a modern language, history and geography. The German gymnasium student takes as many as nine subjects for the abitur, which gives right of entry to university; Russian secondary schools maintain a broad curriculum to the end, and in the USA, the idea of a broad and balanced education continues into higher education.

After the *Crowther Report* (Ministry of Education, 1959), various attempts were made to extend the sixth-form curriculum. In 1961 an *Agreement to Broaden the Curriculum* (ABC) was signed by 360 schools, pledging them to maintain a full range of subjects up to the sixth-form stage, avoid any total separation of arts and sciences, and to keep at least a third of the sixth-form timetable for non-specialist work. In the early 1960s, suggestions for reform based on combinations of 'full' and 'half' subjects as a way of meeting the variety of sixth-form needs were commonly mooted. The pressure for change became greater because the whole nature of sixth forms was changing, particularly in comprehensive schools where, by 1966, as many as half the sixth form might not be taking any A Levels. A number of Schools Council reports (Schools Council, 1966; 1972) pointed to the need for changes and, in response, a variety of 'broadening' devices were proposed, e.g., in 1978 'Normal' (N) and 'Further' (F) Levels.

Yet despite these pressures for change, the pattern of A Level work in our schools has survived. Universities have until recently argued that the proposed changes would be an inadequate basis for degree courses which are already both shorter and more specialized than those in comparable countries. Schools have been concerned that the broadening would lead to the loss of the 'real' standards of academic achievement of which A Level has long served as the custodian. There is a tension between the traditional role of A Levels as a means of university selection and its more recent role as a multi-purpose credential. As Edwards (1983) has pointed out, it is this continuing value as a multi-purpose credential which has reduced the pressure to find general and more directly vocational alternatives.

What marked out the late 1970s and the 1980s was the level of criticism of the existing structure. The period saw mounting tension between those who sought to overhaul the academic curriculum, the 'modernizers' and those who looked to preserve it, the 'traditionalists', or 'Conservative educationalists'. Fierce debate ensued focusing on the impact of proposed changes on quality and standards. Some commentators have seen at the root of such divisions a battle between two competing principles: 'the endorsement of existing inequalities versus the promotion of increasing equality' (Harland, 1991, p.60). The former principle, endorsed by 'traditionalists', seeks to preserve the élitism of the academic curriculum and to maintain the clear division between academic and vocational. The latter, supported by 'modernizers', looks to improve access, participation and achievement in the academic curriculum and to narrow the divide between education and training.

There have been two important shifts which have affected the character of the debate. As education and training have moved up the political agenda, we have witnessed the entry of industry and political parties into the 'secret garden' of education. These groups have joined educators in the debate about the academic curriculum and succeeded in extending the scope of that debate as reflected in the 'alliance's' 'agenda for action'. This greater involvement has prompted the government to take direct control of the power of veto over reform proposals, where previously it lay with the universities and examination boards. The fate of proposals is now more dependent on the attitudes of the Prime Minister and the Secretary of State for Education at the time. The tension between the wider debate and more centralized control has been considerable. It has explained the intensity of the debate about the academic curriculum and the growing dissatisfaction of many in the 'alliance' with government policy.

A key principle in the attitude of successive Conservative governments to the issue of participation and attainment in the academic curriculum has been the preservation of A Levels. This policy was spelt out in *Better Schools*: 'the Government is committed to the retention of A Levels; they set the standards of excellence which need to be preserved' (DES, 1985). It was reaffirmed in the 1991 White Paper with a commitment that 'A Levels will remain the benchmark of academic excellence' (DES/DE,1991a). The pressure from greater student numbers has been met by changing the vocational rather than the academic curriculum with the 'new sixth' being ushered firmly into the vocational route. Increased participation and attainment in the academic curriculum is to be achieved through more students satisfying the standards required to proceed to A Level study and then on to higher education. The government has been quick to highlight the apparent success of this approach in improved examination results in GCSEs and in A and AS Levels.

Successive Conservative governments have stoutly defended this policy and remained firm in the face of the growing consensus for change (Jackson, 1989). The recommendations of the Higginson Committee (DES, 1988) were rejected despite widespread support from many in education, industry, the universities and examination boards. The Government's response to the pressure for change has centred round three key initiatives: the role of Advanced Supplementary courses in broadening the students' curriculum, the role of core skills in furthering this broadening and in linking the academic and vocational curriculum; and the role of the new Advanced Diploma in providing parity of esteem for both academic and vocational courses. The limited nature of these changes and the lukewarm commitment to them has left many groups increasingly frustrated with the lack of meaningful reform.

The events of the past 15 years raise a number of interesting questions. First, why, despite growing criticism of the academic curriculum, has it been able to resist the increasing calls for reform? Second, why has the pressure from the 'alliance' resulted in the restructuring of post-16 training but not in the overhauling of post-16 education? The 'alliance's' 'agenda for action' affords a useful structure to assess the progress of reform in relation to the academic curriculum.

The role of 'academic' courses in increasing participation and attainment rates post-16

Changes in education and society since the introduction of A Levels mean that they have now assumed a much wider role than that of merely preparing students for higher education. There has been a massive increase in the number of students taking A Levels. In 1951, 36,677 candidates were entered for A Level examinations with 103,803 subject entries. By 1991 the number of subject entries had increased six-fold to 695,991. Nevertheless, there has been considerable concern about A Levels focused on two particular phenomena: the small percentage of the age cohort who gain access to the academic curriculum, and the sizeable wastage and failure rate in that group by age 18. Access to A Levels is limited to approximately 25 per cent of the age cohort with only 14 per cent of the cohort gaining two or more A Levels. On average 30 per cent of those who take an A Level fail to receive a pass grade in that subject. Such figures underline how A Levels, originally designed to act as a filter mechanism to identify those from the grammar and independent sector who were suitable candidates for degree courses, still largely fulfil this purpose 40 years later. The essentially norm-referenced examination system created maintains the standard of successful candidates and regulates their number.

As Ball notes, 'it is a bold (or foolhardy?) nation that thinks it can afford to fail at 18 nearly one-third of those identified at 16 as academically most able' (Ball, 1991b), and the unsuitability of A Levels for a large sixth-form population has brought increasing pressure for change. The CBI report *Towards a Skills Revolution* (CBI, 1989) set new targets for increased student attainment post-16 at NVQ Level 3 or its academic equivalent. The 1991 White Paper (DES/DE, 1991a) referred to one in three young people entering higher education by the year 2000. Yet there is little indication of how this target will be met under the present system. The target also conflicts with the government's reaction to renewed anxiety about those 'middle attainers' who attempt A Levels. Many institutions complain of problems coping with a greater proportion of students for whom the transition from GCSE to A Level is proving difficult (SEAC, 1989b). Some institutions have sought *ad hoc* solutions such as the use of AS examinations as stepping-stones to A Levels. The Secretary of State, concerned about the large number of youngsters failing to gain any recognition for two years of A Level study, asked SEAC for advice on the possibility of resurrecting an Intermediate or 'I' Level examination between GCSE and A Level (MacGregor, 1989). The government was swift to condemn the use of AS examinations for such purposes and appears to have lost interest in the problem of large groups of youngsters failing the 'rigorous' academic route. John Major has recently set a new tone in the debate on standards when he noted 'if the transition from GCSE to A Levels is causing difficulties, we [the government] must level GCSE up, not *lower* A Level standards' (Major, 1991). This is an interesting riposte to the 'alliance' criticism of the mismatch between the post-16 academic curriculum and pre-16 education.

A coherent curriculum and qualification system

Much concern has focused on the consequences of the split at 16 between an 'academic' route for an élite minority and a 'vocational' track for the rest, what Sir Claus Moser has called a system designed to separate 'the academic "sheep" from the vocational "goats"' (Moser, 1990, p.16). The reform of the vocational route from the mid-1980s focused attention on the 'divided' system, throwing into sharp relief the extent of the gap between the vocational route and the academic curriculum, with its different content, style of delivery, assessment and end routes. It brought a consensus among the members of the 'alliance' on the need to narrow the divide in standards and status between the two routes but this consensus has broken down over the measures that might be taken. The main division again concerns the method of bridging the gap: whether it is possible through incremental, piecemeal reform or whether more drastic restructuring is required. The Government has favoured an incremental approach which has resulted in a series of attempts to broaden the academic curriculum. Spurred on by the need to take the political initiative the Government has focused on a number of key developments.

The first attempt at reform saw the introduction of Advanced Supplementary (AS) Levels (DES, 1984a) designed to allow A Level students to broaden their studies. The government emphasized that the new examination was of the same quality and standard as A Levels (DES, 1987). Kenneth Baker, Secretary of State for Education, predicted the norm for all A Level students would soon be a '2+2' programme of two A Levels and two AS Levels. The announcement of the new examination in *Better Schools* (DES, 1985), without recourse to any pilot or feasibility study, was unexpected. It confirmed the growing power of the Government over the academic curriculum and its commitment to preserve A Level standards. The Conservative Government has persisted with AS courses as the key to broadening the academic curriculum despite evidence of problems over their status and take-up (DES, 1989a). A SEAC survey in 1989 revealed initial confusion over the status of AS Levels and their use in many institutions as a stepping stone to A Levels

(SEAC, 1989a). Problems over the acceptability of AS Levels for university entrance continue to affect take-up rates (HMI, 1991b), and there is little sign of the Government's '2+2' programme becoming a reality.

The need for careful consideration of the 'academic route' was re-activated by the publication of the Higginson Committee Report (DES, 1988) which recommended five 'broader but leaner' A Levels and more 'balanced programmes of study'. The Higginson Committee went far beyond its original remit and argued that only by thorough overhaul could the academic curriculum meet the needs of students. The Report drew particular attention to the lack of breadth, the need for more active learning, the potential of modularization and the need for a set of principles to improve A/AS syllabuses. Its radical proposals explain why the Report was the most widely supported of any reform proposal over the past 15 years. The Report's rejection proved a watershed in a number of ways. It is strongly rumoured that rejection only came following the last-minute personal intervention of Margaret Thatcher. Siding with the leading representatives of the Headmasters' Conference (HMC), she rejected the recommendations on the grounds that they would have an adverse impact on academic standards. In rejecting the recommendations, the Government re-affirmed its support for broadening through AS Levels. This episode highlights the continuing influence of the independent sector over the academic curriculum. Though numbering only 7 per cent of all schools, they cater for 20 per cent of traditional sixth formers and nearly 30 per cent of all sixth formers studying three A Levels. The Government decision to seek the advice of the independent sector led one observer to remark that given the sector's opposition to A Level reform 'it was a bit like consulting Ronnie Biggs on law and order' (Duffy, 1989). The impact of the rejection of Higginson set the agenda for future reform, for as SEAC noted 'for the foreseeable future the exam [A Level] must remain as the "gold standard" and any reform must find its way round this fixed point' (SEAC, 1989b). This led to the exploration of different reform routes to bridge the divide with many of those in favour of incremental reform channelling their energies into changes in teaching and learning styles and the development of core skills. For others, rejection strengthened their conviction that the way forward was through radical redesign.

In part as an attempt to regain the political initiative after the summary rejection of Higginson, the incorporation of core skills into both academic and vocational courses was publicly broached by Kenneth Baker (Baker, 1989). They were welcomed as a means of bridging the gulf between academic and vocational courses, thus allowing all young people to develop common competences. Their appeal was that core skills related not just to content but also to process. They offered the possibility of broadening the narrow content approach at A Level through new teaching and learning styles. Hopes rose when John MacGregor asked SEAC to investigate core skills at A and AS Level and the possibility of credit transfer between academic and vocational courses. The proposals were immediately attacked by the 'traditionalists' for making things 'easier for the best and harder for the rest' (Jewell, 1990). As Lawson shows in Chapter 7, progress on the delivery of core skills, both within and across academic and vocational courses, has been slow. Despite NCC's strong support for core skills to be an integral part of the academic curriculum and its work with NCVQ to establish equivalences, the Government in the 1991 White Paper (DES/DE, 1991a) and in recent consultative papers sees core skills as at best an additional qualification in numeracy, communication and possibly information technology.

The most recent attempt to bridge the academic/vocational divide was unveiled in the 1991 White Paper *Education and Training for the 21st Century* (DES/DE, 1991a; 1991b). It is based on a new Advanced Level Diploma superimposed on current post-16 qualifications. A Levels remain as 'the benchmark of academic excellence' and those reaching the appropriate level in academic and vocational qualifications receive the Diploma. The proposal has been widely attacked as inconsistent in claiming that the divide can be eased while existing qualifications are maintained. Those in the 'alliance' have been particularly scathing and the approach has been dismissed as 'merely papering over the cracks in the present system' (Ball, 1991c).

Criticism of the cosmetic nature of many incremental proposals and dissatisfaction with the lack of real progress has led to renewed interest in more radical solutions. The design of solutions has been influenced by scrutiny of post-16 systems in other countries with increased interest in the French Baccalaureat, the German Abitur, and the SCOTVEC model in Scotland. The main appeal of these systems is that they allow greater flexibility between education and training, thereby lessening the divide between academic and vocational routes. Modularization is also seen as a vehicle for narrowing the divide. The possibility of future links between academic and vocational courses through common modules for A, AS and BTEC students was raised in the Higginson Report. Pilot work, frequently linked to developments in core skills, has been promoted and supported by TVEI and has involved LEAs working with examination boards to devise innovative modular schemes. Modular solutions have been incorporated into radical proposals, the most influential being the IPPR report (Finegold *et al.*, 1990) which advocates a unified system of education and training leading to a single 'Advanced Diploma' or

'British Baccalaureat'. The proposed Diploma is modular in structure with designated core modules for all in various domains. The report has influenced the thinking of several groups, such as the Royal Society of Arts, the Labour Party and the Liberal Democrat Party.

Whichever route or option is proposed, key questions remain, most notably how to ensure parity of esteem between academic and vocational routes and qualifications. At present the vocational track is perceived as second-best. As Sir Christopher Ball has commented: 'So long as most of the able and highly motivated, fast-learners choose an academic, A Level route at 16, while the slower learners, late developers and the unmotivated are offered vocational courses, parity of esteem is neither likely nor appropriate' (Ball, 1991b). Some argue that the root of the problem lies beyond education in the wider cultural, economic and political advantages which accrue to those who take the academic route (see, for example, Chitty, 1991; Moser, 1990; Skilbeck *et al.*, 1985). A Levels continue to have great 'currency value' and, although vocational qualifications have great 'use value', their 'currency value' is unclear. Employers are more likely to choose academic over vocational qualifications (Raffe, 1985) reaffirming the cultural superiority of academic 'knowing' over vocational 'doing'.

Many believe that true parity will only come when there is no particular advantage in taking one route over another. That will entail the acceptance of real change by educators and a revolution in long-standing cultural, economic and political prejudices. It will also require the political will to countenance such change. Many question, given the current lack of progress, whether this political will exists. The more pessimistic suspect that the Conservative Government's education policy seeks to preserve and extend the divided nature of the post-16 system (Hargreaves, 1989; Lawton, 1989; Reid, 1991). They warn that the National Curriculum threatens to reinforce the separated education and training systems and strengthen the deeply grooved hierarchies of 'the educated', 'the trained' and 'the workers' (Ainley, 1990). They fear that it will soon be clear who fits into what groove by the age of 14.

The revolution in teaching and learning

Much concern has been focused on the impact of teaching and learning styles on student motivation in academic courses. Advanced Levels, and to a lesser extent AS courses, have been criticized for their narrow subject specialism and undue emphasis on content over process. This, coupled with the predominance of terminal assessment, has resulted in a reliance on didactic teaching and passive learning which is often inappropriate for student needs (HMI, 1989a; SEAC, 1989a).

The last decade has witnessed a re-evaluation of the processes of learning particularly in pre-vocational and vocational courses. TVEI and GCSE developments, in particular, have introduced student-centred pedagogy, often growing from new local consortia arrangements. Their success has fuelled demands for similar flexible and imaginative approaches to learning and assessment in the post-16 academic curriculum. This has created pressure for A Levels to come more into line not only with their vocational equivalents but also with GCSE and higher education courses. It has brought criticism of the academic curriculum as an anachronism, out of step with the rest of the education system (Ball, 1991b).

The strength of such demands, coupled with increased disaffection with the present system, has encouraged many examination boards and subject associations to support such initiatives. Examination boards have been involved in the development of regional, modular syllabuses, such as the Wessex (Rainbow, 1990) and UCLES schemes, and many subject groupings are developing innovative syllabuses such as the Cambridge History Project and SMP's new 16–19 mathematics course. The result has been a series of initiatives to develop and trial new and revised A and AS syllabuses across subjects and regions. The developments are *ad hoc* and uncoordinated and there are problems over national accreditation, but they offer a basis for future syllabus reform.

The calls in the Higginson Report for a reduction in content and more varied assessment to make A and AS syllabuses more attractive to students were taken up by SEAC which moved to give direction to the many uncoordinated syllabus initiatives. A and AS Levels might remain but their nature could be fundamentally altered through content and assessment changes. SEAC established a number of committees to investigate and report on A and AS Levels in relation to core skills, vocational linkage, progression from GCSE, assessment patterns and suitability. The result was a list of principles which SEAC envisaged would govern and rationalize all A and AS syllabuses by 1994 (SEAC, 1991a).

Such proposals and actions have met fierce resistance from 'traditionalists' who view the factual content of A/AS Levels as one of the major strengths of the academic curriculum and believe that any change would entail a loss of academic rigour and a reduction in standards. The root of the 'traditionalists' opposition was encapsulated in a comment from the right wing Centre for Policy Studies that 'British education has lost its way by going for equality at the expense of quality' (Anderson, 1991). John Major also entered the debate with his call for 'getting GCSE back to being an externally assessed exam, which is predominantly written' (Major, 1991).

The search for coherence

For many critics of the current situation, the main anxiety has been about the lack of overall coordination and continuity in 16–19 policy. As HMI reported:

> there is no one curriculum for 16–19 education and no overall curriculum rationale. There is a wide variety of providers, sponsors and exam bodies; the two most important influences on course content are the requirements of H.E. and of employment (HMI 1989b).

The academic and vocational are separate routes controlled by different agencies; 'different kings rule in different parts of the jungle' (Harland, 1991, p.54).

Two major groupings have been identified in this jungle (Haffenden, 1990). The 'education sub-group' dominated by the DES rule the academic curriculum, deciding on policy which is administered by LEAs and examination boards and delivered largely through schools and colleges. The 'training sub-group' composed of the DE and the DTI rule the vocational and work routes, deciding on a policy which is administered by TEED (formerly MSC and TA), TECs and NCVQ and examining bodies such as BTEC, CGLI and RSA, and delivered largely through FE colleges and YT schemes. The divide between the two groups which results in major differences in content, assessment, course structure and institutional organization between academic and vocational routes, is a severe obstacle to continuity and progression in 16–19 policy. The divide is reinforced by the markedly different perspectives of the two groups. The 'education sub-group' is deeply influenced by its senior partner, the DES, whose involvement with compulsory education in schools leads to an emphasis on academic excellence and selective examinations. The group's 16–19 thinking is framed by the need to preserve the standards and rigour of A/AS Levels as determined by the requirements of first degree courses. Vocational education and training is regarded as second best for the less able or those unwilling to pursue an academic education. The 'training sub-group' is influenced by its links with employers and the world of work and sees education as requiring a vocational element for all in preparation for employment. The group's 16–19 thinking and policy is concerned with bringing education and work closer together and introducing vocational aspects into all courses, including A Levels. This has led to calls for a recognizable 14–19 curriculum as embodied in the TVEI approach.

The lack of coordination and agreement between and within the groups has been responsible for many of the unsuccessful attempts at change. The authority of the DES within the 'education sub-group' has made real reform almost impossible. It has ensured that 16–19 policy has been dominated by the needs of the academic curriculum and by the desire to maintain at all costs the primacy of A Levels over other qualifications. Even during the period 1976–87, when the 'training sub-group' was in the ascendancy, the 'education sub-group' was able to resist attempts to introduce vocational aspects into academic courses and to bring academic and vocational courses closer together. Underlying the resistance was a fundamental belief in the superiority of the academic curriculum. As Ainley notes, 'even during the vocational phase of education policy too many programmes for relating education to work and for developing training were perceived as being "for other people's children"' (Ainley, 1990, p.121). Many continue to believe vocational aspects are for the less able and have no place in the academic curriculum where they threaten standards. Since 1988 and the demise of MSC, the DES has tightened its grip over 16–19 education. Some commentators argue the 'education sub-group' are using the National Curriculum to further marginalize the gains of the 'training sub-group' at pre-16 and to broaden or increase the divide at post-16 between academic and vocational routes (Jones, 1989; Lawton, 1989).

Conclusion

The academic curriculum has resisted the 'alliance' challenge to reform post-16 education and training over the past 15 years. A Levels continue to dominate and drive the post-16 system. This resistance has been successful because of weaknesses in the 'alliance' and in its reform approach and because of the power of those who seek to preserve the academic curriculum. The 'alliance's' favoured approach to reform has been piecemeal, incremental change. However, this reinforces the tendency to view academic and vocational routes separately. The result has been short-term reactive policies which tinker with rather than reshape the academic curriculum. As a consequence, 'new policies have had only limited impact on the implicit assumptions within which education at 16 plus is carried on' (Reid, 1991, p.36). This problem has been exacerbated by weaknesses and divisions in the 'alliance' which contrasts with the strength of those who seek to retain the academic curriculum. They are a long-standing and well-organized coalition comprising 'Conservative educationalists' in government, the DES and the independent sector, the very groups who control and dictate policy in the academic curriculum. They have used this authority to slow up and deflect the 'alliance' challenge. They have been strengthened in their actions by support from many employers and the general public who still champion the academic curriculum.

The coalition presence has had a number of important outcomes. The coalition's lack of interest in vocational education and training has left the 'alliance' unopposed to reform the vocational route. However, the strength of the coalition has dissuaded the 'alliance' from making a similar sustained challenge to the academic curriculum, particularly A Levels. Meanwhile, the 'Conservative educationalists' have been sufficiently strong to ride the policy tensions created by the 'alliance' in government circles (Jones, 1989). They have mobilized skilfully their forces, including successive prime ministers, to defeat proposals centred on the 'agenda for action'. Their success has encouraged them to challenge 'alliance' ideas further through the National Curriculum.

The prospects for future reform of the academic curriculum are not promising. The incremental approach is flawed and unlikely to achieve results given the forces of inertia working against it. This was highlighted in the rejection of the Higginson Report despite widespread support for it outside government. Meanwhile, the divisions fostered by the National Curriculum threaten to reinforce rather than reduce the divided nature of post-16 education and training. The only hope of real change lies in tackling the assumptions which underpin the present system. As Sir Claus Moser notes, 'we need a leap in the quality and vision of our education debate and in the educational goals we set ourselves' (Moser, 1990, p.6). The one body capable of giving such a lead is the government. The major political parties have ducked the issue to date, perhaps mindful of the impact on electoral fortunes. It is nothing new. 'Contemporary events have made the problem more difficult and there is no certainty whether education should be primarily vocational, moral or cultural'. These are the words of Aristotle. The same dilemma lies at the heart of the post-16 debate.

CHAPTER 4

From Pre-Vocational to GNVQ

Neil Stock and Graham Conway

Introduction

Provision for students deemed to be unsuitable for or uncommitted to existing 'academic' or 'vocational' provision post-16 has been a constant issue for those concerned with planning post-16 education. In the 1930s, some schools were already running 'alternative' sixth-form courses, particularly for girls. In 1939, the *Spens Report* argued that 'a wide liberty should be left to the schools in the choice and arrangements of these courses' while noting that many schools were offering 'preliminary vocational training of such a kind that the pupil will recognise its value for the next stage of life' (Board of Education, 1939, p. 166). The *Crowther Report* (Ministry of Education, 1959) did not make consideration of alternatives to the traditional sixth form a central concern. Although a chapter was devoted to the subject, no specific recommendations were made and the discussion was largely concerned with the 'needs' of girls considering entering occupations such as nursing and teaching. However, Crowther foresaw that a rise in the 'trend' of those staying on would create the need for a more urgent consideration of the issue.

The increase in the numbers of non-selective schools and sixth form colleges with no conventional entry requirements to post-16 education and the rise in youth unemployment meant that, by the end of the 1970s, about a fifth of all school sixth formers and a third of those in their first year sixth lacked the conventional academic qualifications and intentions (Edwards, 1983). Moreover, an increasing proportion of students post-16 were choosing to move to FE Colleges, and many were following 'non-traditional' courses. Debate arose as to whether the conventional programme for such students of retakes in 'O' levels or CSE was appropriate. Critics of the inappropriateness of the routes available pointed out that examinations designed for particular ability ranges do not necessarily become easier because candidates are older or study them for a longer period of time. Researchers (Vincent and Dean, 1977) pointed to the general lack of success of young people re-taking Ordinary Levels, one study noting that 40 per cent of sixth formers taking four Ordinary Levels as the basis of their one year course failed them all (DES, 1979). However, there has been considerable difficulty in developing 'alternative' sixth-form curricula, partly as a result of the strongly instrumental view of staying on post-16 frequently expressed by sixth formers and their parents. Schools and colleges have therefore shown an understandable reluctance to limit access to opportunities associated with 'high status' academic qualifications.

The immediate response from the 'traditional' school examination boards to the inappropriateness of the existing programmes for the new clientele was the introduction of the pilot Certificate in Extended Education (CEE) in 1972, based on an 'academic' interpretation of the new students' needs. At the same time, the 'vocational' examination boards introduced more vocationally-oriented qualifications, e.g., City and Guilds Foundation Programmes and later 365 courses for these students. In the late 1970s, the provision was viewed from two different perspectives. From one direction, the Keohane Committee (DES, 1979) advocated the retention of CEE with some amendments. From the other, a review undertaken by the FEU led to the publication of the document *A Basis for Choice* (ABC) (FEU, 1979), also known as the Mansell Report, which advocated a pre-vocational course consisting of core, vocational and job-specific studies. The two reports, in their different recommendations, reflected the competing interests prevailing at this particular time. The Keohane Report was supported by the 'education' sector, i.e., the CSE examination boards, the Schools Council and the teacher unions. It supported an approach emphasizing single-subject courses building upon and extending the academic curriculum of the secondary school. The Mansell Report was supported by the Further Education sector and reflected the interests of the 'industrial trainer' lobby in its emphasis on technical work-related knowledge.

It was the recommendation of the FEU group which received support from the DES and the go ahead was given to pilot schemes based on the principles of 'ABC'. Such programmes began to mushroom in the early 1980s, most of the schemes including common elements with options. ABC itself provided a framework for one-year courses, the components of which were generally grouped under three main headings:

- Core studies – learning common to vocational preparation (mainly basic skills such as numeracy and communication).
- Vocational studies – learning particular to a given vocational sector.

●Job-specific studies – learning particular to a given job sector.

For schools and colleges, such programmes were a real challenge in terms of staff development, curriculum organization, and planning. A report from a Norfolk working party emphasized that courses of this type would require a multi-disciplinary and cross-curricular approach more typical of further education. It argued that 'Shared teaching between further education colleges and schools will be necessary if real progress is to be made. It is recommended that new courses are carefully planned with the fullest co-operation between schools, F.E. and the LEA' (Norfolk County Council, 1981). In keeping with the Norfolk Working Party's findings, many schools entered into collaboration with FE colleges to provide the more vocational parts of the one-year sixth programme. Such experiences were incorporated into City and Guilds '365' courses that were increasingly being offered to sixth-form students in the early 1980s.

The Certificate in Pre-Vocational Education

In May 1982, the DES published a proposal to introduce a new 17+ qualification called the Certificate of Pre-Vocational Education (CPVE). Pilot schemes started in September 1984, with full implementation from September 1985. Its introduction was heralded as a major curriculum innovation as the CPVE 'framework' was different in structure, content and methods from subject-based courses previously offered. Initially the framework comprised:

●Core (made up of ten components including numeracy and communication).
●Vocational studies at introductory, exploratory and preparatory levels in five areas.
●Additional studies (which included sport, GCSEs, etc.).
●Learning through practical experience (including a minimum of 15 days work experience).
●Counselling, guidance and review.

The CPVE framework consisted of an integrated approach to the delivery of the curriculum, both in linking the core with vocational areas and in integrating the 10 compulsory core areas. In terms of delivery, the traditional teacher control of the curriculum was challenged through the concept of negotiation and the call for activity-based, experiential learning. It also introduced a formative profiling system based on core competence statements through which students could negotiate their level of achievement.

CPVE was initially planned as a one-year course available for 16–17 year olds of all abilities. However, many schools introduced it with a pilot group of their less able sixth formers and there was a tendency from the start for it to be associated with a low-achieving intake. Moreover, there was little acceptance of CPVE as a valid qualification and its credibility was not helped by the lack of clearly defined progression routes from CPVE onto other academic or vocational courses. Many centres had difficulty achieving integration between the 10 components of the core and between the core and the vocational areas. A national evaluation in the academic year 1987–8 highlighted many of these problems and recommended changes which were implemented in September 1989 (BTEC/CGLI, 1988). The changes included a revised set of core objectives, a more flexible timescale allowing completion over a period of up to two years, and a reduction in the time requirement for CPVE, allowing CPVE to be followed in conjunction with a wider range of other qualifications. Such changes have been welcomed by schools and colleges who now have the flexibility to offer a pre-vocational programme to all their post-16 students. This is particularly the case in schools that had embarked on TVEI extension, for the CPVE philosophy has much to commend it as a framework for all. In 1991, 10 per cent of CPVE students also took A Level but unfortunately many schools still used the CPVE framework only for those of lower ability and combined it with programmes largely based on GCSE retakes.

Concern about this provision still centres around two issues: What added value do the students gain from staying on for one extra year and following such a programme? Does such a programme give students access to a full entitlement curriculum? One has to be a little wary in trying to answer these questions. The added value to a student of following a programme consisting of GCSE retakes and CPVE may be in the form of gaining a year's greater maturity in a relatively 'safe' educational environment. However, if one is measuring added value purely in terms of academic achievement and progression opportunities, then doubts must be raised about the educational adequacy of such a provision. Although data are notoriously difficult to collect, it seems that a great many students fail to improve their GCSE grades significantly.

Again, one has to be careful when assessing the degree to which students following the typical one-year provision of CPVE and GCSE retakes have access to a full entitlement curriculum. Many agencies have been using the term 'entitlement' in different ways. Nevertheless, a degree of consensus is emerging over the 'elements' of entitlement to which all young people should have access to assist their educational, personal and vocational development. Many LEAs, as they have embarked on TVEI post-16, with its contractual requirement to provide an 'entitlement' for all post-16 students, have identified the key elements of a student's post-16 experience. One such interpretation includes:

skills, such as numeracy, communication, problem solving;
experiences, such as off-site activities, practical activities;
contexts for learning, such as group work, enterprise;
dimensions, such as guidance, RoA (ALEP, 1989).

In cases of the best CPVE practice, such elements of entitlement are integral to the provision. However, in many cases CPVE is contained within a provision largely dominated by GCSE retakes. The one-year sixth becomes a year in which students aim to improve marginally their achievements in 'core' GCSE subjects in two terms. Any free time is largely unplanned and, consequently, many elements of a student's entitlement fall by the wayside.

The 1991 White Paper

The Government has recognized, as part of the continuing national debate on 16–19 education and training, that compared with the academic route 'the vocational route is potentially far more important in increasing the numbers who benefit from post-16 and higher education' (DES News, 1990b). The vocational qualifications on offer to students staying on at school for an extra year will need to have greater currency, and the provision available in such courses will require greater rigour and fuller entitlement elements in order to attract a wider cohort of students and to ensure progression.

Moreover, if the 'world class targets' referred to in Chapter 1 are to be met, many of the new students will not start their post-16 education or training careers in traditional 'academic' or 'vocational' courses. They will require courses which allow them 'to keep their options open. They want to study for qualifications which prepare them for employment in a range of related occupations and keep open the possibility of going into higher education' (DES News, 1991). The first steps along the way to reformulating the provision on offer in this area was taken in the run up to the publication of the White Paper in May 1991. In his last speech as Secretary of State, Mr. MacGregor said:

> BTEC and other vocational courses can provide a high quality alternative route....
> They are indeed already doing so on an increasing scale and I believe this needs to

be much more widely recognised. Vocational qualifications offer a thoroughly valid alternative route which should have equal esteem to the academic 'A' level route (DES News, 1990a).

In December 1990 it was announced that schools would be encouraged from September 1991 to offer BTEC Firsts – work-related studies in subjects such as business and finance and that the examining body City and Guilds was to take sole responsibility for CPVE and strengthen it as another stepping stone to higher level qualifications (DES News, 1990c). CPVE was seen as in need of rigour and clearer progression opportunities. It was stressed that there must be cooperation between BTEC and CGLI such that the 'improved CPVE will be accepted as a standard entry route to BTEC Nationals'.

City and Guilds responded by announcing in June 1991 that CPVE and Foundation Programmes would be replaced by the Diploma of Vocational Education, which would be piloted in schools and colleges from September 1991. The Diploma of Vocational Education will cover the 14–19 age range and will have three levels: Foundation, Intermediate and National. The Foundation level at Key Stage 4 gives the student the opportunity to develop personal and social skills and to acquire skills and knowledge within a broad vocational context. Post-16, the Diploma of Vocational Education will operate as both a one- and two-year programme at Intermediate and National Levels. The work will be closely aligned to General National Vocational Qualifications (GNVQs), the Intermediate to Level 2 and the National to Level 3. If students are to achieve an Intermediate Diploma they must, as a minimum requirement, have completed one Introductory Module, one Exploratory and five Preparatory Modules, 'competent unaided under supervision', as well as completing 15 days minimum work experience. The higher level of attainment now being required, particularly in the Preparatory modules, is designed to enhance progression routes for students and therefore make the Diploma more attractive than CPVE to the whole ability range.

The response

The intention is to extend the range of services offered by school sixth forms and colleges so that young people face fewer restrictions on what education or training they choose, and where they take it up. Thus structures are being created which will allow students, irrespective of the institution attended, to study a combination of courses accredited by academic or vocational qualifications.

The problems facing institutions as they decide how to respond to these developments vary according to the scale and style of their post-16 provision. Institutions providing 'dedicated' post-16 provision, particularly where they have substantial numbers of staff with recent industrial experience, will be able to draw on their prior work in this area and offer a comprehensive provision. Schools, particularly those with relatively small post-16 rolls, will be faced with difficult decisions over which provision to choose and whether the new provision will have greater currency and potential for progression than CPVE.

BTEC Firsts will look an attractive proposition to many as they already have credibility and provide a well-defined progression route on to BTEC National. They are, however, vocational courses and require a vocational commitment on the part of the students intending to follow them. They will be particularly appropriate for the students who, as a result of initiatives such as TVEI, are now reaching the sixth form with a clearer idea of what they want to do in life. Moreover, in a situation where a Minister has spoken of giving schools pre-16,

> ...more room to manoeuvre within the basic framework of the National Curriculum... (and the creation of) two parallel streams – the academic and the vocational – from halfway through Secondary School so that children can concentrate on what interests them.... In other words, the whole system will move towards a greater degree of specialisation with a far greater commitment to vocational education (*The Daily Telegraph, 6 November 1990*)

the demand for them is likely to increase. However, there are other general issues that will need to be considered by schools and colleges intending to offer this qualification. First, because BTEC Firsts are vocational courses, they require a wholly different set of teaching expertise, especially with the advent of NVQs and the emphasis on vocational competence. The issue of the vocational experience of staff and effective links with local industry and commerce will therefore be critical. Second, BTEC Firsts are an integrated programme and institutions will need to identify how the study elements will be interrelated and how common skills will be developed. This will present difficult coordination problems if students are to take part of their course in school and part in an FE college. Third, vocational courses require specialized accommodation and items of equipment, limiting the range of BTEC First courses which schools will be able to offer.

The City and Guilds' new Diploma of Vocational Education retains many of the features found to be attractive with CPVE: formative assessment, active learning and broad vocational training. It now offers the possibility of providing differentiation between students which should increase its credibility when using the accreditation for progression onto higher-level courses. However, the Diploma too has its drawbacks. First, many institutions will be disappointed to see that students will need to focus far more closely on one vocational cluster if they are to achieve the five preparatory modules they require for accreditation. Students can include up to two generic modules which may offer the flexibility for retaining the vocational breadth that CPVE supporters valued. Secondly, the whole area of accrediting core skill achievement remains confused. City and Guilds are hoping that they will be able to bring the Diploma in line with GNVQ but at what level is still open to debate. This raises the third major issue: to what degree will the Diploma successfully differentiate between students and will this be accepted by employers and gatekeepers of full-time vocational courses as a means of meeting entry requirements that usually demand, for example, four GCSEs?

GNVQs

Thus, whilst BTEC Firsts and the Diploma of Vocational Education both offer possibilities for institutions looking to provide an appropriate programme for students, there are still several issues that need resolving. The success of these new moves is going to be heavily dependent on the response to GNVQs. The Government wishes to create GNVQs as a new third route into employment and HE. GNVQs will provide a broad foundation within a vocational area from which students can progress to NVQs in particular occupations or to higher levels of education. They will be distinctive from occupationally-specific NVQs, cover broad occupational areas, be modular, and designed for use by students in colleges ('and if appropriate in schools'), who want to study for vocational qualifications related to a range of occupations and who do not want to limit their choices too early. NCVQ is currently working on pilot GNVQs. Unlike NVQs, GNVQs will not be based directly on occupational competence but will focus on the skills, knowledge and understanding that underpin a range of NVQs within a broad occupational area. The process is proving to be difficult because employer lead bodies are used to issuing NVQs for very specific competences in a particular type of employment. The more generic attainments envisaged by GNVQ do not easily fit this model.

It is proposed that GNVQs will consist of a fixed number of units covering the fundamental skills, principles, and processes of an occupational area. All the units for a particular level of GNVQ will be of the same degree of complexity. This will help people understand the system and programme design and allow students to interchange units between different GNVQs. It is proposed that in the pilot GNVQs, starting in September 1992, a Level 3 GNVQ will be awarded on the achievement of 12 vocational units of attainment. These will consist of eight mandatory units plus four optional units chosen from a specified range. Students would also have to achieve attainment in five core skill units. These will be acquired and assessed as an integral part of the 12 vocational units described above. Students will be encouraged to gain units beyond 12 to add to and broaden their range of achievement. It is suggested that 18 units (equivalent to 3 A Levels) could become a normal target for high achievers. By encouraging students to gain additional units to the basic 12 required for a GNVQ, considerable flexibility will be added to the qualification system. It is suggested that the units for a Level 3 GNVQ should be comparable with the demands of A and A/S levels. One unit of attainment at GNVQ will equate with one third of an A/S , or one sixth of an A Level. Thus a Level 3 GNVQ will be equivalent in 'weight' or coverage to two A Levels.

GNVQs at Level 2 will consist of six mandatory units. These will be derived from the mandatory eight units at Level 3, but will be less demanding than Level 3. This arrangement might allow scope for schools and colleges to run common programmes in the first year for Level 2 and 3 awards, if they so wish. Level 2 awards also require the incorporation of National Curriculum attainments at KS4 Level 7 upwards. Students working towards Level 2 awards will also be encouraged to take extra units or possible GCSEs or other studies.

It is assumed that Level 2 GNVQs will normally be achieved after about one year and that Level 3 GNVQs will normally be offered in two-year programmes. NCVQ does not award qualifications itself; it accredits the qualifications of awarding bodies which meet specified criteria. In the initial phase starting in September 1992, GNVQs will be awarded by BTEC, City and Guilds and the RSA Examination Board.

The major issue is going to be the credibility of these new awards. Will they gain sufficient credibility among young people, employers and those who control admission to further and higher education to become a genuine alternative route? The scale of the challenge is considerable and has met with failure so far. As the leader in the *Times Educational Supplement* (13 September 1991) presented it, 'It is not enough for Mr Eggar (Education Minister) or even the Prime Minister to say that vocational qualifications must have equal esteem with an academic equivalent *if no one believes it...*'

Major problems are likely to arise as a result of the conflict between the political and the educational role of GNVQs. The political impetus for their creation sees their main function as a way to bridge the academic/vocational divide while at the same time keeping intact the 'gold standard' of A Levels. The immediate attention has been therefore on establishing the higher levels of the qualification and, in particular, on the relationship between GNVQs, A Levels and progression to opportunities in higher education. Discussion has focused on how to achieve differentiation at the higher levels in a route designed to be assessed on the basis of competence. However, their main educational role will be to act as the assessment route for youngsters who have traditionally been viewed as the least successful in academic terms. For the majority of youngsters taking this route, attaining the Intermediate Level will be a considerable achievement and, if the new rigour applies, many will not achieve this. The issue will be again to what extent do the new arrangements provide better opportunities for such youngsters

On the one hand, the 1991 White Paper appears to be advocating a system whereby students have access to a combination of academic and vocational qualifications and can move easily between them. On the other, it seems to be designing separate systems of qualifications that have little common ground between them. At the heart of this distinction is the Government's determination to leave the 'gold standard' of A Levels untouched. Of course, things are changing all the time, but as this chapter is being written there appear to be significant structural differences between the different routes.

Academic	The New Bridge	Vocational
Advanced Levels AS examinations	Diploma of Vocational Education GNVQs	NVQs
Content-based mainly on knowledge and understanding	Content-based mainly on standards of attainment	Content-based mainly on competencies
Assessment 20 per cent maximum for course work, 80 per cent written exam	Assessment – continuing assessment in institutional contexts	Continuing assessment – using appropriate methods in an appropriate workplace or simulated working environment

The potential for confusion and the creation of barriers by the markedly different approaches taken is considerable.

Conclusion

The tensions, lack of detail and inconsistencies raised by the 1991 White Paper have thrown those charged with managing and delivering post-16 education into a state of confusion. They accept that the CPVE/GCSE retake provision existing in many institutions has little to offer students in terms of progression or currency. Most will acknowledge the opportunities presented by the City and Guilds' new provision and by BTEC. They also welcome the statements made in the White Paper regarding the promotion of equal esteem for vocational and academic qualifications and clearer and more accessible paths between them.

Against this lies the preservation of the A Level 'gold standard' and the dichotomies between the proposals for academic and vocational qualifications discussed above. Add to this the fact that several bodies, the Labour Party (Labour Party, 1991) included, have advocated plans (of varying degrees of sophistication) for a unified qualifications system which would be modular in structure and replace A Levels and vocational courses, and the confusions and fears of making rapid (but much needed) changes to the post-16 provision are total.

Only events will tell whether the quality, breadth and currency of the provision will reach the standards demanded by a modern society, or if yet another generation of students will be doomed to an inferior and inappropriate provision.

CHAPTER 5

Teaching and Learning Styles
Peter Mayne

Writing in 1990 Anne Jones declares:

> Now more than ever before, managing schools is about managing change...rapid
> and escalating change...so the shape of our schools and colleges is...changing; the
> way that they are organised, the way teachers and students work... (ED, 1990).

The rhetoric of change has long been on the lips of those seeking to
direct post-16 education at the system level. This chapter will consider
how far this culture has succeeded in effecting change where the business of education is transacted, in the classroom. Has change occurred
there or is there a cruel discontinuity between the change rhetoric and the
processes of an educational system whose 'most remarkable feature ... is
its capacity for continuity and stability in the face of efforts at change'
(House, 1979).

Opportunities and impediments

Nowhere has the imperative for change post-16 been more urgent than in
the 'way teachers and students work'; without it change elsewhere will
be no more than cosmetic. Yet, in spite of major changes in the politics
of educational control, the power to effect this change remains with
teachers, whose responsibility 'lies first and foremost in the domain of
pedagogy...the setting of learning objectives, the planning of learning
experiences and the assessment of students' achievements'
(Leicestershire LEA, 1988). Teachers, therefore, already possess a key to
unlock the 16–19 curriculum and to achieve many of the 'alliance's'
goals for relevance and breadth, without the need to 'tarry on the magis-
trate' (a phrase used by Elizabethan Protestants who waited for government action – in vain).

Traditionally, however, pedagogy has been undervalued. No clear science of teaching developed in this country and as a result 'our approach
to educational theory and practice has tended to be amateurish and prag-

matic' (Simon, 1981) In the absence of professional consensus on how students learn, teaching has developed as an individual and isolated activity. This exists in an attenuated form post-16 where teachers prize their professional autonomy. As a result, pedagogy has been low on the agenda and at the margins of legitimacy for discussion, even where teachers share a teaching group (Mayne, 1988).

The spirit of the 1980s has added further impediments to pedagogic change. Market forces and accountability to students, parents and management are keenly felt and impact on classroom practice. At a time when the educational establishment encouraged teachers to reflect on the quality of student learning, course aims beyond the syllabus and cross-curricularity, these contra-pressures exerted a powerful restraint. The expansion of the A Level cohort should, prima facie, have produced pedagogic change; it has conversely led to pedagogic retrenchment and to teaching to the exam.

By the early 1990s there were signs that GCSE, TVEI and Records of Achievement had powerfully influenced curriculum experience pre-16. The pace of change had caused teachers – in extremis – to work together in devising new approaches in the classroom and to recognize that they 'develop professionally when they refine their knowledge about pedagogy by observing and reflecting upon their experience in organizing students' learning in classrooms' (Leicestershire LEA, 1988). By contrast, 16–19 work has remained in something of a time warp. Hence, whilst syllabus content and resources were common topics for departmental discussion, classroom process was not. A study undertaken in the mid 1980s failed to locate any whole-establishment discussion on this topic (Mayne, 1988). The profile of pedagogy as an issue of professional concern appeared to decline in a negative correlation to the increase in the age of students encountered.

Inside the 'black box'

In the past, admission into the 'black box' of the post-16 classroom has been notoriously difficult and little empirical research has occurred there. The survey work and published inspection reports of HMI, however, provide a useful source of information and those on the subject of vocational and academic courses alike make for depressing reading. The following are typical comments:

> Generally the teaching was competent but uninspiring. Teaching styles tended to rely on chalk and talk, dictation, instruction and description. The pace is generally slow, students are rarely stretched and seldom involved in a classroom activity other than that of note-taking and filing handouts (HMI, 1984b).

> Some teachers...spent too much time simply transmitting information...which students could have acquired themselves from textbooks or discovered through well structured and planned assignments (HMI, 1987a).

Whilst about half the teaching and learning observed by HMI in FE during 1989–90 was good and most of it at least satisfactory, where poor practice existed it was 'characterised by too much uninspiring talk by the teacher; poor management of classroom time; inadequately planned lessons, and a lack of relevant activities which challenge the students and hold their interest'. The Senior Chief HMI noted, 'There is scope for colleges to carry out more quality control and assurance of the range and effectiveness of learning activities' (HMI, 1991a).

A Level work is widely seen as a marker of quality in the system, but its status lies in the accredited outcome rather than in any intrinsic qualities in the learning process:

> ...in more than half the lessons seen in sixth forms students spent a considerable proportion of their time as passive recipients of information (HMI, 1988b).
>
> ...the principal objective of many staff and students alike, was the provision of what they regarded as a 'safe' set of notes for revision purposes, and there were examples of teachers engaging in monotonous and extensive exposition, dictating notes or requiring notes to be copied from the blackboard, and of students taking a wholly passive role (HMI, 1988a).
>
> Some of the teaching took place in the constant shadow of the examination with a narrow concentration on essay and context questions to the exclusion of other activities, which had the effect of shrouding the vitality of literature in an air of gloomy retribution (HMI, 1986).

The prevailing criticism is that where didactic approaches dominate, a classroom ethos develops which 'encourages passive attitudes in students who often appear to lack involvement in or enthusiasm for the subjects being studied' (HMI, 1984a). The lessons of good practice elsewhere show that 'good teaching and effective learning necessarily employ a variety of approaches in which students are actively involved, and in which they become progressively more responsible for their own learning' (Warwickshire LEA, 1989).

One study, undertaken in 1986 (Mayne, 1986), has sought to lift the lid off the 'black box' in order to glimpse A Level classroom process: to describe the pedagogic repertoire of the teachers and the incidence of particular teaching strategies and, more importantly, to assess the extent to which A Level teachers actually think pedagogically. Drawing from empirically derived data, its conclusions support HMI's picture of A Level classroom experience. Emphatically, students in this study experienced a pedagogy which lacked variety and was didactic and whole-class in orientation – the traditional safe route to achieving examination success. Teachers and students perceived their classroom experience differently, with teachers claiming significantly higher frequencies of non-directive and group strategies than were perceived by their students. They dictated notes, lectured and presented themselves as providers of factual information to a far greater extent in the eyes of their students than they themselves would admit and they were at variance with their students on the frequency with which they involved students in lessons, even at the level of asking questions and promoting class discussion. Students perceived lower levels of group work, collaboration and student presentations. They saw their teachers interacting with individual students and small groups much less than their teachers indicated. The teachers appeared singularly unable to describe with precision either their repertoire of strategies or the frequency with which particular strategies were employed. The study concluded that in an environment where process was a far less important consideration than content coverage or percentage pass-rates, and where discussion on methodology was rare, teachers were insufficiently practised in articulating their pedagogy.

The teaching and learning process has appeared, however, on the agenda of other groups. It has long been fashionable for such groups to speak of the knowledge explosion and of 'replacing the idea of a sufficient initial education with an emphasis on life-long learning' (RSA, 1991). Hence it follows that on any post-16 course 'the way that people learn...becomes more important (ED, 1991b). Learning to learn and practising those competences in a wide variety of contexts is an important strand in core skills literature. Practitioner and professional judgements have found support also in work on learning style theory in the United States which raises issues of access to effective learning and demonstrates that equality of opportunity for learners cannot exist within a narrow pedagogic repertoire:

> Students more or less continuously exposed to classroom cultures that fail to acknowledge their learning style needs experience a loss of self-esteem, stress, a decline in motivation, a sense of failure and alienation. A balanced diversity of styles is essential if all our students are to emerge from school as healthier, more rounded individuals (Selby, 1989).

At the same time as teaching and learning remain acutely urgent issues for schools and colleges to address, there is evidence that the process of review is under way and that pedagogy has been slipped onto the agenda of professional discussion.

Teaching and learning styles: confronting the taboo

It is, of course, very difficult to isolate the reasons why a particular teacher reviews her methodology. It seems a fair supposition, however, that the causes will be an amalgam of personal and professional factors – a new teacher in the department, changes in college management, attendance on a course, a chance dialogue with a student – and that these factors will interact one with another. One vehicle for pedagogic change has been teacher participation in curriculum initiatives. In this section five such initiatives are considered:

- New provision – CPVE;
- TVEI;
- New methods of accreditation – BTEC;
- Profiling and Records of Achievement;
- Enhancing mainstream subject teaching.

Whilst these are described separately, the reality of their influence is compound.

Many curriculum initiatives in the 1980s occurred as a result of collaboration between teachers from a number of colleges. This originated in collaborative approaches to '17+' and minority subject provision, continued through TRIST (TVEI-Related INSET) groups to TVEI 'clusters'. The opportunity for teachers to work beyond the confines of the single institution, to gain an overview of developments and hands-on experience of curriculum development has delivered mutual professional development and a potent engine of change. It has shaped a generation of middle managers exercising cross-curricular roles which has brought direct influence to bear on teaching and learning styles.

New provisions and the transferability of practice

A significant feature of curriculum development in the 1980s was the way in which ideas and practice were transferred between course teams and institutions of different types. In this way ideas and practice originating in newly developed provisions, particularly in YTS and Vocational Preparation, gained currency and application beyond the discrete provision and in curriculum contexts very different from their origination. Collaboration between schools and FE Colleges in developing City and Guilds 365 and CPVE programmes brought many teachers into contact with literature produced by the FEU. At a time when very little was being written from a school perspective about teaching and learning styles post-16, the FEU provided stimulus for teachers to review their repertoire of teaching strategies and to engage in dialogue about pedagogy with their immediate colleagues.

Many teachers involved in the delivery of both CPVE and A Level courses in schools began to apply ideas gained from CPVE to their mainstream subject teaching. Hence they saw the advantages of unitizing their courses, providing explicit pre-unit guidance on the content, the skills to be developed and the methods of course delivery and assessment. They appreciated the potential for enhancing curriculum experience in mainstream studies through the use of collaborative group work and the development of study and presentation skills. Most significantly, they saw the benefits of teacher-student reviews and student self assessment.

Drawing on the FEU document *Towards a Framework for Curriculum Entitlement* (FEU, 1989b) one group of A Level teachers chose to define the rights of learners in the form of questions which any A Level student was entitled to have answered (ALEP, 1989):

What will I learn on this course?
How will I learn it?
How will I be treated on this course?
What will I be able to do as a result of this course?
What will I be able to do after I have completed this course?

These student-centred approaches share a philosophy of learning with Records of Achievement and Flexible Learning and have been important in sowing the early seeds of change.

The Technical and Vocational Education Initiative

TVEI, which began its pilot phase in 1983 and its extension from 1987, has been a major catalyst for curriculum development post-16. One feature has been the widespread adoption of the concept of post-16 entitlement. This has breathed life into discussion of post-16 curricula at LEA, area and institutional levels, and has had a powerful influence on change in approaches to teaching and learning in the classroom. Despite initial professional disquiet, TVEI, far from vocationalizing and centralizing the curriculum, has been responsible for empowering classroom teachers to engage in initiatives in their immediate curriculum areas which have contributed to a humanizing of the curriculum, emphasizing the importance of personal and social skills and active and flexible learning in 'real life' situations. TVEI has been instrumental in challenging teachers in the post-16 sector to review their classroom practice, legitimizing and impelling teachers to discuss pedagogy.

'Active learning' has been a key TVEI objective. It developed from a fairly narrow construct of enrichment and experience of work, enterprise and residential courses, into a curriculum principle applicable to mainstream study – even to 'the gold standard'. Higginson (DES, 1988) wrote:

> A Level should...aim to whet the appetite for active learning. Project and practical work, simulation, working with others, discussion and oral presentation can all offer opportunities for students to practise relevant skills and can jolt them out of a passive attitude to learning.

It is no coincidence that TVEI supported institutions under Schools Regulations to run BTEC programmes.

Flexible Learning has a similar paternity and is seen as a vehicle for developing autonomous and personally effective young people. Initially surfacing as 'Supported Self Study' (SSS), Flexible Learning has been marketed energetically by the Department of Employment as a strategic force for change. SSS may have been born of necessity – as in its use in Northumberland to maintain access to a full range of A Level subjects – but its curriculum virtues (Waterhouse, 1983) are clear in quality learning materials which compare favourably with Open University units in their attention to developing flexible but ordered approaches to study.

All LEAs were required to address flexible teaching and learning styles within their proposals for the 16–18 phase of TVEI Extension from 1988. A network of regional Flexible Learning projects was launched in 1989 and the Flexible Learning Framework in 1991 (ED, 1991b). The latter comprises three interdependent processes managed by the teacher: the interaction of the student and the learning resources, student-tutor 'partnership' and monitoring and assessment. Each of the eleven schemes within the national *Managing Flexible Learning: The Role of IT* project (1990–93) involves post-16 students. One scheme is exploring flexible learning as a means of assisting student progression from a variety of pre-16 science backgrounds to A Level chemistry, the running of mathematics workshops, the management of personal studies in history and the development of library and information skills within mainstream geography studies.

Accreditation – Business Technician Education Council

One of the most interesting developments of the 1980s has been the emergence of what might be termed the 'BTEC approach to learning' which has produced a qualitative shift in teaching and learning styles as a direct result of accreditation. Although at first exclusively FE in domain, BTEC has latterly taken root in schools.

BTEC is a validating as well as an examining body, which approves colleges to offer its courses through a process of initial submission and moderation based on its principles of active student-centred learning, vocational realism, work- related assessment, and team delivery. These courses therefore combine two pedagogic features previously lacking from the post-16 scene. First, the course must be taught by a team who are expected to meet regularly to coordinate the integrated process of learning across the course elements. The very structure of the provision therefore demands a collaborative approach to classroom process. Second, unlike A Level, BTEC is concerned with the quality of the process of learning itself. BTEC insists that students learn in an active, student-centred way through case studies and integrative assignments, and that they have access to a broad range of learning resources including information technology. As with CPVE, where teachers are engaged in delivering a number of programmes, their experience of BTEC has influenced their pedagogy elsewhere.

Profiling and Records of Achievement (RoA)

Recording achievement has been a further stimulus to reflection on post-16 classroom process which could not have been foreseen at its origination. RoA began as 'profiles' designed for low attainers poorly served by existing forms of accreditation and the 1984 RoA pilot schemes targeted the 16+ school leaver. RoA are now used with students across the ability range post-16. Whilst initially profiles and RoA were seen as whole-programme instruments, essentially pastoral, summative and documentary, their value to many teachers is curricular and formative; their 'not-so-hidden agenda' is in changing learning styles through the operation of the formative process. Where 'curriculum time' is to be used for student-tutor and peer reviews, change in classroom management must ensue – reviews simply can not coexist with a predominantly teacher-driven pedagogy. Review requires the pre-publication of clear assessment criteria, it facilitates dialogue on individual learning needs and enables feedback on the learning experiences planned by the teacher. The RoA process is a feature of formative assessment in BTEC and in modular A Level courses such as Wessex.

TVEI has been instrumental in selling the RoA concept and more recently in developing student action plans (ED/NRA, 1991). Again these have an application in the classroom in providing a framework for student-teacher dialogue and opportunities for differentiated tasks and outcomes. History staff in one sixth-form college use action plans to support students engaged in a personal study which lasts for over a year and accounts for 25 per cent of the A Level final assessment. Action plans are used to break down this daunting assignment into a series of short-term targets which are reviewed in one-to-one or small group tutorials. This has great value in assisting students to acquire learning skills.

Enhancing mainstream studies

Curriculum organization post-16 and the language of articulation has undergone significant change in the past decade. Whilst opportunities have been maintained for students to experience rigour and depth in their studies by acquiring specialist knowledge and skills, breadth is now a widely accepted principle of curriculum planning post-16. Students study programmes, rather than combinations of subjects, and have an entitlement to certain experiences. Considerable energy has been harnessed to counter over-specialization and narrowness in academic and vocational programmes post-16. Traditionally the favoured method of achieving breadth was through 'enrichment' activities often encompassed within programmes of general studies. Yet 'the history of attempts to deliver breadth and relevance post-16 as "additionality" is strewn with a litany of failed good intentions' (Mayne, 1990) and the preferred method now is through the enhancement of mainstream studies. This rests on the acceptance that examination and teaching syllabuses are not synonymous, and therefore reform of teaching and learning need not await Board or ministerial decree.

Although HMI (1991b) found that in many colleges 'there was no expectation that departments would produce schemes of work' and where they did 'rarely went beyond quoting the Advanced Level examination syllabus', this is not universally so. Where departments have prepared schemes of work which extend beyond the syllabus, they are an exceptional aid to the delivery of varied teaching programmes. At their best they describe methodology and access to resources and environments, as well as opportunities for differentiation and extension work and the development of cross-curricular skills, themes and links. Where schemes are prepared collaboratively, pedagogy is assured of a high profile in professional debate and as a result the curriculum experience of students is considerably enhanced. The excellent HMI document *Experiencing A Level: Aspects of Quality* (1987b) provides examples of good practice in teaching programmes which go far beyond the narrow confines of the syllabus and offer point and relevance to students.

The TVEI Extension has contributed greatly to collaborative schemes for subject enhancement, two examples being the A Level Enhancement Project in the North West and Leicestershire's Post-16 Subject Development Programme. Here groups of teachers are released to produce materials and ideas designed to assist in the delivery of entitlements through the enhancement of mainstream studies. The Leicestershire scheme has supported 17 subject teams over two years and the materials are being trialled widely. Examples of 'enhancements' include the development of oral presentation skills in physics, the use of film and portraiture as sources in history, and exemplar study units and self-assessment materials in a range of subject areas. Where teachers have seen the benefits of an approach which empowers them to improve the quality of student experience and learning, they have been prepared to absorb the opportunity costs of searching for lighter and more appropriate syllabuses.

Conclusion

The teaching and learning experienced by many students 16–19 has continued to reflect that characteristic resilience to change described by House (1979). Discussion of teaching and learning post-16 has, until very recently, been a rare feature of professional dialogue between teachers who exercise a degree of autonomy in curriculum delivery which is astonishing in the light of the whole-institutional debate and development which has characterized change in so much else of the corporate life of schools and colleges. However, there are encouraging signs that 'the way teachers and students work' is changing post-16 and the power of teachers to effect change through pedagogy is gradually being recognized.

CHAPTER 6

Records of Achievement

Paul Kennewell

Introduction

In February 1991, the Government issued the National Record of
Achievement (NRA), free, for use on a national 'pilot' basis.
Accompanying the NRA was a guidance booklet, *Recording
Achievement and Planning Individual Development* (ED/NRA, 1991).
Both these documents offered substantial support for the principles
which had emerged during preceding development work, both in terms
of the National Record being proposed and the processes recommended
to underpin its production. There was a re-statement, in modified form,
of the broad purposes of the recording of achievement that had first
appeared in the DES's policy statement of 1984 (DES, 1984b). An
accompanying letter, jointly signed by the Secretaries of State for
Employment and Education, commended the use of the NRA for all
learners, whether they be in education, training or employment and made
an explicit claim for the motivational value of the recording of achievement in terms of developing a commitment to 'life-long learning'.

To some observers the emergence of the NRA may have come as
somewhat of a surprise, not only because of the massive resources implications, but also because there had appeared to be a lack of Government
support in the preceding two years, particularly from the DES, for the
broad concept of Records of Achievement (RoA) outlined in the guidance booklet. This chapter will examine the developments which have
led to the establishment of the NRA, the role of the 'alliance' in establishing RoA on a national level and their relationship to wider 'agendas
for action'.

Developments in the Recording of Achievement and the role of the 'alliance'

When analysing the emergence of RoA three broad development phases can be distinguished, incremental in nature, which have helped shape the contemporary situation. These developments have their roots in both education (pre- and post-16) and training, there having been an interplay of influence between various initiatives with the 'alliance' playing a crucial role, particularly in the latter stages.

The first stage of development was largely concerned with the summative aspects of RoA. These refer to the production of a final document, orientated to an external audience, indicating the student's performance across a wide range of activity. The provision of such a summary document emerged initially as a reaction to the inadequacies of traditional examinations in meeting the needs of the new body of students introduced by the raising of the school leaving age (ROSLA) in 1973. The early profiling schemes can therefore be seen, in many cases, as grassroots responses to the practical problems of providing worthwhile educational experiences for these students. The reporting on a wider range of experiences and achievements was seen to have a dual function in that it acted as a source of motivation for those who were more likely to fail in the academic domain, thus providing a 'curricular activator' (Stansbury, 1975) while also providing 'a wider and more useful range of achievements' (Broadfoot, 1986b) for consideration by the external audience.

To a large extent, therefore, the emphasis on the summary reporting of a wide range of achievement was seen as an antidote to the over-reliance on an external examination system which served to produce a de-motivated section of the student community and the results of which, often expressed in grades, gave little indication of the students' capabilities.

The FEU's *A Basis for Choice* (FEU, 1979) was an important influence in shaping the early formats of summary documents and informing the underlying principles of the recording of achievement process. In exploring the possibility of rationalizing the proliferation of pre-vocational courses, the ABC study group recommended a graded profile which would report on the student's competence in a number of defined skill areas. The recommendations reflected the FEU's belief in the transferability of skills, and inspired a number of profile schemes, notably the City and Guilds 365 Basic Abilities Profile and the competence-based profile developed for the CPVE.

CPVE's requirements incorporated a student-centred formative assessment process, based on the concept of 'negotiation', with the emphasis on positive achievement in terms of the acquisition of specific skills and knowledge. This reflected the second stage of development of RoA which laid emphasis on the perceived value of the formative processes seen to underpin the recording of achievement. These processes include: student involvement in the assessment of their own learning; dialogue and regular review; identification of strengths and weaknesses; the iden- tification of future learning needs; the collation of evidence; and the recording of achievement across and beyond the curriculum. Students have increasingly been seen as central to this process and it has become generally accepted that to be effective the formative process should be an integral part of the teaching and learning experience, supported by the policy and organization of the institution.

The central role of the student in the formative process was enhanced through the work of the Education Support Grant (ESG) pilot schemes established by the Government in Autumn 1985. The pilot schemes ini- tially concentrated on developments for those students in the compulsory sector of schooling but were extended in 1988 to include RoA post-16 and to consider issues of continuity and progression. They were intended to establish good practice and to address issues identified in the 1984 policy statement. Evaluation of the schemes was carried out by the Pilot Records of Achievement in Schools Evaluation (PRAISE) team (Broadfoot et al., 1988; 1991). In addition the Records of Achievement Steering Committee (RANSC) was set up by the Government to oversee the initiatives and to produce recommendations from the initial pilot work.

The Steering Committee produced its report in 1989 (DES, 1989b) proposing a national framework for the full implementation of RoA for students in compulsory education. This framework supported the princi- ples underlying the formative process and advocated validation and accreditation procedures which would ensure the credibility of RoAs. It was argued, 'It is essential...that the assessment, recording and reporting processes should be established, monitored and evaluated with the linked aims of achieving quality and credibility' (DES, 1989b, p.14). This emphasized the importance of whole-institution policies on the recording of achievement and signalled the move away from 'initiative' status. The PRAISE team in their second evaluation report commented on the increased tendency of the RoA principles to 'lose the label' and become transformed into 'generic definitions of professional competence' (Broadfoot et al., 1991, p.75).

Throughout this development phase it was recognized that the forma- tive process could also act as a catalyst for change in the learning environ- ment (Law, 1984). If fully implemented, it could be seen as a key ingre- dient in curriculum management and design, providing a structured framework for a continuous evaluation of the curriculum and teaching methodology and an agenda for the setting of objectives related to students' needs. The recording of achievement, incorporating diagnostic assessment, leads, it is argued, to curriculum review and change, prompting a more student-centred agenda. It is significant in this respect that the processes involved in the recording of achievement are central to the Flexible Learning Framework (DE, 1991).

RoA thus has significance as a potential mechanism for change in the learning environment. This was recognized at an early stage of its development by the members of the 'alliance'. The MSC (later TA, now TEED), a key partner, provided a major impetus for the development by establishing the recording of achievement as one of the central elements of its major vehicles for change, the TVEI and the YTS.

At the time of its introduction, TVEI was unique in being a centrally managed curriculum project which had a substantial amount of resources available in support of curriculum change and evaluation. TVEI has formed a significant platform for the development of RoA, particularly as schemes were contractually bound to deliver them (see Gleeson, 1987). The early TVEI pilot schemes were limited to cohorts of students, making it difficult for the recording processes to be fully embedded in whole-institution procedures and philosophies. Furthermore, there was a tendency to report on the 'TVEI curriculum' rather than the whole curriculum of the student (Baines *et al.*, 1989).

The extension of TVEI to all pre-16 students and to post-16 students has increased the pressure for a whole-institution response. In TVEI post-16 explicit links have been made between RoA and the Entitlement Curriculum. Definitions of the entitlement vary but all have the common categories of skills, experiences, contexts (e.g., group work, enterprise) and dimensions (e.g., guidance, recording achievement) (Spencer, 1990). The recording of achievement process provides some of the dimensions of entitlement and can accredit the skills and experiences. The notion of entitlement has also been linked to the concept of student 'empowerment'. The recording of achievement provides a means of auditing the curriculum whereby the student, through the review process, maintains an overview of entitlement across and within their programme of study.

The YTS, introduced by the MSC in 1983, similarly required the provision of continuous assessment, guidance and support and the recording and review of progress and achievement. Trainees were to be issued with a YTS Record of Achievement and Certificate on completion of their training. These were to be supplemented by a log book of personal experiences and a trainee diary. The previous FEU development work on profiling was significant in influencing the implementation of the YTS, as the philosophy and format to a large extent met the MSC's requirements. This development helped acquaint employers, as managing agents, with the processes underpinning the recording of achievement. The criteria for the provision of YTS has now changed. Managing agents now have to accredit training within the National Vocational Qualification framework and to issue trainees with the National Record of Vocational Achievement (NRoVA).

The Department of Employment has thus provided explicit support, including resources, for the development of the recording of achievement from an early stage. It is worth exploring the reasons behind this support and to see how it is perceived as a central part of the broader 'agenda for action'. Around the development of Records of Achievement there has emerged a surrounding philosophy, indeed rhetoric, which has presented them as having significant potential to change the process of education and training. At the institutional level they are said to have the potential to promote more effective student-centred teaching and learning styles which are responsive to individual need and which can enhance the quality of the learning experience. They are also seen as providing a climate which may enhance the relationship between the provider and the learner, through the process of regular review and discussion. This in turn has the potential to reduce the alienative influences of traditional assessment and thus encourage greater participation and improved levels of achievement. At the individual level, Records of Achievement are seen as motivating the learners and giving them 'a sense of achievement and the confidence to set targets and go on learning throughout life' (Jones, 1990). They can aid 'the missionary role of school teachers (in) inculcating respect and love for future learning' (Ball, 1991b). In addition, the recording of achievement is seen as assisting the learners to 'assess accurately their own qualities and capabilities, to perform appropriately and effectively across a range of roles and situations' (Jones, 1990) and thus more adequately preparing them for their role in adult life.

The importance of the 'alliance's' commitment to the development of Records of Achievement was evident during the third development phase which was dominated by apparent Government prevarication about the future of RoAs. This was seen particularly in the DES response to the RANSC report and the subsequent SEAC consultation exercise on Records of Achievement. SEAC found 'strong and widespread support for the nationwide use of Records of Achievement in schools...along the lines described in the RANSC report' (Letter from Halsey, SEAC to Secretary of State, July 1989) and positively recommended their full implementation. The headlines of the time, 'Government "snub" for records of achievement' (*Times Educational Supplement*, 6 October

1989), reflected the view that these recommendations had been ignored with the Government adopting a minimalist view and concentrating on the reporting of the National Curriculum under section 22 of the Education Reform Act (ERA). The perceived failure of the Government to support the 1984 policy statement 'checked the growth of RoAs and the head of steam for development, while LEAs and schools examined the implications' (Broadfoot *et al.*, 1991, p.3).

The publication of the CBI report *Towards a Skills Revolution* (CBI, 1989) was crucial at this stage in providing a rallying call for the 'alliance' to support the development of the wider concept of Records of Achievement as recommended in the RANSC report. The Training Agency, particularly through TVEI, was called upon to carry the development forward. The report proposed that:

> One national system of Records of Achievement and action plans should be used both in schools and employment, pre-16 and post-16. This would require a coming together of school records with the National Record of Vocational Achievement and the embracing of records and action plans within one profile. All young people would then be treated equally, irrespective of the route of their learning and the profile would emphasise that structured learning should take place throughout the 14–18 age range and beyond (CBI, 1989, p.22).

In addition, in relation to Records of Achievement, the report called for enhanced careers guidance, the introduction of individual credits, the assessment and recording of transferable (core) skills and the provision of broad based qualifications. These measures, alongside the notion of employers as 'Investors in Training' and the creation of a 'real market' for training, were presented as vital in helping meet the 'world class targets' of education and training set by the report.

These proposals gave explicit recognition to the 'alliance's' view of the relationship between Records of Achievement and the broader 'agenda for action' in providing a bridge across the academic/vocational divide and assisting in the 'revolution in expectations, standards and the delivery of education and training (which) must take place' (CBI, 1989, p.9). Similar support came from other 'alliance' partners; for example the TUC in their document *Skills 2000* (TUC, 1989) and from the statutory bodies such as the National Curriculum Council (NCC, 1990a).

The CBI report was significant as it provided a blueprint for subsequent developments and acted as a political lever within the Government and, in particular, the Department of Employment. In response, the Training Agency issued in December 1989 draft guidance on the use of Records of Achievement in TVEI. As a result of the consultation the document *Guidance for those Managing TVEI: Recording Achievement and Planning Individual Development* (ED/TVEI, 1991) was issued and gained widespread support representing as it did a vindication of the principles contained in the RANSC report. The preface to this document reflected the CBI view of the role of Records of Achievement:

> Beyond school, in higher and further education and in the world of work and training, RoAs are being used more and more to maximise the effective development of individuals. It is recognised that individuals need to take control of their own learning needs in order for the country to compete in both European and world terms and Records of Achievement are essential tools for the task (ED/TVEI, 1991).

The Guidance was also significant in that it introduced, in a more explicit form, the concept of Individual Action Planning as an integral feature of the recording of achievement process, consolidating the third stage of development.

The use of the term 'Individual Action Planning' had its origins in training provision. It was a feature of Employment Training (ET-Action and Personal Training Plan), Youth Training (YT-Category B trainees, i.e., special needs) and integral to NRoVA. From this early narrow focus the process gained wide support as being applicable for all students and trainees involved in education and training. This support came from bodies such as the National Curriculum Council (NCC, 1990a; 1990b), the Further Education Unit and other 'alliance' partners.

The Training Agency was particularly significant in 'pump-priming' the development through TVEI by making the inclusion of Action Planning a contractual requirement of the extension proposals and by the establishment in 1989 of 47 Youth Development Projects (YDPs) with three years funding. There were two broad clusters of YDPs, those concerned with building bridges between academic and vocational experiences and those concerned with Individual Action Planning (see ED, 1991c).

The process of Individual Action Planning may be seen to have two broad functions. The first is concerned with curriculum management enabling an individual to monitor their learning and development needs in either education or training. This involves target-setting arising from the formative assessment cycle and periodic review of the curriculum opportunities being offered, with adjustments being negotiated where necessary. The second is concerned with transition management, assisting the individual in the transfer from one phase of education or training into another or into employment.

In Action Planning associated with transition management, an essential pre-requisite is that the counsellor or counselling agent should be independent of the learning opportunity provider. This requirement has focused particular attention on the major role of the Careers Service in providing information, advice and independent counselling and guidance, acting as the 'honest broker' at transition stages. Indeed, the position of the Careers Service has been under scrutiny, with pressure to move it away from direct Local Education Authority control and for more Training and Enterprise Council involvement (DES/DE, 1991b). The development of Action Planning has thus been seen as a major element leading to the provision of enhanced careers guidance by widening the horizons of individuals and thus encouraging them to take more actual responsibility for their education and training.

The next stage of development in terms of Records of Achievement and Action Planning is likely to be a more explicit, if not formal, link with Training Credits, already a feature of some of the pilot schemes (see TVEI, 1991). Training Credits represent an alternative way of funding Youth Training. Individuals are issued with a voucher representing a monetary value when they leave full-time education at the age of 16 or 17 and, through the guidance process, they devise a training plan usually aimed at NVQ Level 2 or above (except in the case of special needs trainees). Public money is thus routed through the individual. This is claimed to have a dual effect. It gives individuals more choice and control and raises their motivation to train while also developing a competitive 'market' for training provision (DES/DE, 1991b). Here then, clear links are made to the need to raise participation and standards and to encourage employers to provide effective training.

The Training Agency has also been pro-active in developing Higher Education awareness and use of Records of Achievement. The main vehicle for this has been through the Enterprise in Higher Education (EHE) Initiative launched in 1987 (TA, 1989). This has encouraged project institutions, again through contractual incentive, to provide formative assessment procedures and a Record of Achievement, thus offering opportunities for continuity and progression, in terms of process and product, for students entering higher education. Projects have also developed learning contract mechanisms as a form of curriculum management action planning (ED, 1990). Through the work of the EHE projects, the YDP project at Sussex University and the experience gained from attempts to widen access generally, there have also been efforts to encourage the use of Records of Achievement as a means of devising alternative admissions criteria for higher education.

Records of Achievement are thus now part of the national agenda, are permeating many areas of education, training and employment and have maintained 'alliance' support throughout their development. However, a number of issues remain which may have an influence on the potential of Records of Achievement.

Issues

There still remains a credibility problem in terms of 'end-user' acceptance of the summary document as an aspect of the selection process. In terms of use in the employment selection process there is still a lack of awareness, particularly among smaller employers, of the potential role of RoA (Broadfoot *et al.*, 1991). There is a similar problem in terms of Higher Education's acceptance of RoA. Some progress has been made through projects under the aegis of EHE and YDP, and the efforts of LEAs in organizing liaison conferences (Wigan Education Department, 1990) has led to some acknowledgement of RoAs on application forms for HE. However, a tension persists between the confidential nature of the UCCA/PCAS reference and the principles of the recording of achievement. Admissions policies vary between and within higher education institutions and amongst admissions tutors – the 'gatekeepers' – there is often limited knowledge of RoA (Gretton, 1990). This, coupled with the increasing tendency not to interview students, means that RoAs still face a credibility problem. This problem may well be exacerbated with the proposed Ordinary and Advanced Diplomas providing another 'hurdle' in the selection stakes with possible consequent effects on participation rates and student motivation.

Individual students and trainees are keenly aware of the importance placed in our society on the terminal products of achievement. This has helped create an instrumentalist attitude to education/training which is difficult to counter. There is a sound rationale for the formative process of RoA, accepted by educationalists and promoted by its advocates. However, evidence demonstrates that the clients, in the form of students and trainees, are not as convinced (see, for example, Broadfoot *et al.*, 1988; Whiteside, 1990). This creates problems in the practical implementation of RoA and may mitigate against the perceived motivational advantages.

The recording of achievement has been demonstrated to have a positive impact on teaching and learning styles in spite of difficulties such as the content-laden nature of many A Levels. It is generally felt that courses with continuous assessment provide more 'natural' opportunities for incorporation of RoA processes. However, the trend towards courses at AS/A Level with a significant continuous assessment element may be halted by the Government view that coursework should be set at a maximum of 20 per cent. Adherence to the 'gold standard' of A/AS Level and the equating of rigour with terminal assessment does not provide a conducive climate for the development of integrated RoA processes. The assessment of core skills as an integral feature of post-16 programmes of study (NCC, 1990a), another potentially integrative measure, appears to have slipped from the agenda, now being narrowly equated with achieving GCSE or its equivalent in mathematics and English in the consultation paper on Ordinary/Advanced Diplomas. These messages emanating from central government do little to encourage the incorporation of RoA processes into classroom practice.

There still remains a lack of clarity about the relationship between the NRA and the NRoVA and there is a divergence of principles between the two. At the present time we thus have two separate national systems of recording, both instituted by central government. The relationship of the NRA to the new Diploma is also unclear. The apparent lack of coherence at the centre still remains problematic.

The development of Action Planning as a pro-active element of the RoA formative process has been welcomed by members of 'the alliance' and has had beneficial consequences. However, the emergence of Training Credits and their relationship to the Action Planning process will require close scrutiny if the operation is not to be diverted to a mechanistic exercise through which student ownership is lost. In the present economic climate, we must be careful not to raise expectations for them to be dashed on the rocks of recession – the current retrenchment in terms of training provision underlines the need for caution.

CHAPTER 7

Core Skills 16-19

Tony Lawson

One aspect on which the 'alliance' would seem to be in general agreement is the contribution of core skills to a broad and balanced post-16 curriculum. Both the education and training partners in the 'alliance' have been keen to promote the concept of core skills as a way of resolving some of the dilemmas which they face in promoting a more coherent post-16 curriculum. At first glance, it may seem that the widespread acceptance of the need for core skills represents a vindication of the concerns and solutions adopted by the vocational wing of the 'alliance'. However, many reform-minded educationalists have readily embraced the concept because it appeared to offer an opportunity to widen the post-16 curriculum whilst retaining the strengths of the traditional A Level system. Nevertheless, there remain key differences of opinion over the issue of how core skills are to be incorporated within the post-16 qualification system, both between vocationalists and educationalists, and amongst educationalists themselves.

The development of the core skills concept

Though the idea of a 'core' has usually been associated with the vocational wing of the 'alliance', the notion that there should be 'a common core' or 'common learning outcomes' or 'common skills' has been discussed in educational circles for some time. Indeed, the introduction of the National Curriculum can be seen as a vindication of the idea that there ought to be a core of educational experience for all children and the extension of the idea to the 16–19 phase as a natural development of this principle.

As far back as 1959, the Crowther Report (Ministry of Education, 1959) was rehearsing many of the concerns of the 1980s and advocating 'common elements...(such as) religious education; arts and music; and physical education' and 'complementary elements...designed to ensure the literacy of science specialists and the "numeracy" of arts specialists for post-16 students'. Thus, educationalists have traditionally been concerned to extend the common experiences of post-16 students, though their favoured solutions reflected the dominant ideas of their time.

The current debate concerning core skills however was heralded by the publication of the FEU document *A Basis for Choice* (ABC) (FEU, 1979). In this and subsequent documents, the FEU consistently advocated a core of entitlement for all FE learners which included skills such as communication, numeracy and personal skills, as well as wider themes such as political and economic literacy. The ideas contained in ABC provided the inspiration for much of the innovation in CPVE and BTEC courses.

One of the major developments in the area during the 1980s was the Core Skills Project of 1982 to 1985, initially funded by the MSC in response to the New Training Initiative. In the early development phase of the Youth Training Scheme, an attempt was made to establish a core skills framework, which would attempt to identify occupational competence through the definition of 103 core skills which were common to a number of tasks and which therefore could be transferred from one job to another. Central to the project was the development of a common language of skills, so that skills could be recognized, accredited and therefore transferred from one occupational context to another, thereby establishing the adaptability of the workforce which was the prime aim of the NTI. So, developments in core skills during the early 1980s were to be found in training establishments and FE rather than in schools.

However, in 1989, a speech by the then Secretary of State for Education, Kenneth Baker, to the Association of Colleges of Further and Higher Education (Baker, 1989) catapulted core skills onto the national agenda for change in the 16–19 sector. In the speech, he proposed a curriculum for 16–19 year olds which would incorporate a set of core skills, described as 'competence built on knowledge and understanding'. The impetus was built up with the endorsement of the idea in a variety of reports from a number of agencies. The CBI in late 1989 embraced the idea of 'Common Learning Outcomes' for the post-16 sector (CBI, 1989). Both the TUC (TUC, 1989) and HMI (HMI, 1989b) contributed to the debate with varying degrees of enthusiasm.

With a new Secretary of State for Education, John MacGregor, the pace was quickened with his request of 28 November 1989 that the NCC and SEAC should explore the possibility of including core skills in the study programmes and syllabuses of post-16 Advanced and AS Level subjects. In so doing, they were required to consult with the vocational sector in the form of the NCVQ, the TA (as it was then) and the FEU.

This development of more formal requirements for consultation between the educationalists and vocationalists seemed to herald a new era of cooperation between what were often seen as competing bureaucracies or 'empires'. The publication of the NCC Report *Core Skills 16–19* in March 1990 (NCC, 1990a) and the NCVQ *Common Learning Outcomes: Core Skills in A/AS Levels and NVQs* (NCVQ, 1990b) seemed to cement the 'alliance', as the NCVQ accepted the list of core skills proposed by the NCC and recognized that they constituted a basis for credit transfer between vocational and academic qualifications.

In May 1990, the Secretary of State endorsed the NCC's list of core skills in principle and by July the other player in the game, SEAC, also reported that core skills could be incorporated into A and AS Level syllabuses, with certain provisos. Subsequently, in September 1990, SEAC published its *Draft Principles for GCE A and AS Examinations*, which proposed including the development of core skills within all A/AS syllabuses and the principle that the assessment of core skills will contribute to the final grade awarded (SEAC, 1991a). The official NCVQ response in July 1990 also accepted the feasibility of core skills across the academic/vocational divide under certain conditions. The interested parties then set up a task group of four experts from a range of backgrounds to develop definitions of core skills, statements describing differentiation of performance and a common system for reporting achievement in the core skills. The task group were supposed to report in January 1991, but a year later, no official report had been published.

What are the core skills?

As the idea of a core skills approach to post-16 education developed, various groups have advocated different lists of core skills, depending upon the groups' traditions, interests and objectives. Halsey has noted 'core skills, competences and competencies (have been) used indifferently' with no guarantee that they all were the same in the mind of the user (Halsey in SEAC, 1991b). Nor has there always been a clear distinction made between what might be properly defined as skills, and what the National Curriculum defines as themes. For example, the CPVE core competences included Personal and Career Development, as well as Industrial, Social and Environmental Studies, reflecting their vocational origin. In Kenneth Baker's original proposals for core skills, he specified 'Familiarity with Workplace Systems and Procedures' as one of the core skills needed for training a flexible workforce (Baker, 1989). This again suggested the influence of the vocational part of the 'alliance'. However, by the time that the NCC proposed its list of core skills, which are the ones now generally accepted, Economic and Industrial Understanding had been transferred from the list of core skills to the list of themes which all post-16 students should address (NCC, 1990a).

The NCC list comprised six core skills, divided into those which could be properly applied to all programmes of work post-16 and those which would be more appropriate for some types of subject than others.

The first group of three skills are:

1. communication skills, which cover the ability of students to extract, present, analyse and evaluate information in a wide variety of formats;
2. problem-solving skills, which involve students in identifying problems, proposing and implementing solutions and reviewing the effectiveness of the adopted solution;
3. personal skills, which necessitate an action planning approach to a student's own strengths and weaknesses, with a greater responsibility for managing learning being devolved to the student.

The second group of skills are:

4. numeracy, which includes the interpretation, presentation and application of numerical data;
5. information technology, which encompasses a wide range of data-handling techniques from word-processing to modelling;
6. modern language competence, which covers the ability to communicate in a modern foreign language in both written and oral forms.

The purpose of core skills

Though there has been a general acceptance of core skills as the way forward for post-16 education, the objectives and intentions of the different members of the 'alliance' vary considerably. The importance of identifying the purpose which attached to core skills is that how they are defined and implemented may in part depend on the utility which is attached to them.

Originally, vocationalists attached to the Youth Training Scheme through the MSC saw core skills as facilitating transfer of workers from one job to another during their working lives. The purpose then was to develop a 'highly skilled, technically competent workforce which was also versatile, adaptable and mobile' (Levy, 1987, p.3). The connection between core skills and the needs of industry is an explicit one, with both the CBI and the TUC identifying a need for all students to be equipped to take their place in a modern economy through the acquisition of useful skills. As the CBI reported, 'all education and training provision should be structured and designed to develop self reliance, flexibility and broad competence as well as specific skills' (CBI, 1989).

The NCVQ saw Common Learning Outcomes as the means to raise the status of vocational education and training in order to bring it to the same level as academic education, and to facilitate progression from vocational courses to Higher Education (NCVQ, 1989a). Others stressed the utility of core skills in bridging the gap between vocational and academic education and thus in facilitating transfer between the two types of courses (Holness, 1990).

The HMI and FEU purpose was broader than this, with an emphasis on the acquisition of core skills by young people as a preparation for a variety of roles and to enable them to respond to conditions of change in a positive way. Therefore, HMI was emphasizing not just the needs of the economy, but also the needs of the individual. Core skills were thus seen as increasing the relevance of qualifications to adult and working life (HMI, 1989b).

Following the lead taken by Kenneth Baker, the NCC was keen to incorporate core skills in programmes of study to promote progression and continuity from the National Curriculum into post-16 education and thus ensure greater breadth and balance in the curriculum beyond the statutory leaving age (Burrage, 1991) Subsidiary purposes identified by the NCC included the encouragement of the transfer of skills from one context to another and more informative reporting of student experiences and achievements through Action Planning and a Record of Achievement (NCC, 1990a).

SEAC's concern was more focused on progression in teaching and learning styles, and the perceived disjuncture between the practices encouraged by the GCSE and the traditional approaches adopted in A and AS Level courses. Core skills development then was seen as one way in which significant changes in approaches to teaching and learning could be developed, with students taking greater responsibility for their own learning and the extension of project and group work into post-16 experiences (SEAC, 1990a).

Thus, as the FEU has argued strongly (Stanton, 1990a), there are several different purposes behind support for core skills, and individuals and groups vary in the priority they give to them. The claim that the introduction of core skills has widespread support in principle is a valid one, but whether that support can be mobilized for the specific details of implementation remains to be seen. As the concerns of the vocationalists are not likely to be the same as those of the academics, the potential for disagreement over the final form of core skills provision is real.

The implementation of core skills

The potential for disagreement over the implementation of core skills across the post-16 curriculum is built into the brief which the concerned bodies were given by the then Secretary of State for Education and Science, John MacGregor. In his letter to the interested parties setting out the agenda for development, he stated that,

> it is essential that nothing be done to prejudice the A level standards based upon academic rigour and study in depth. If core skills can be embedded in syllabuses without prejudicing those standards, well and good (MacGregor, 1990).

Moreover, the incorporation of core skills into specific A and AS syllabuses had to be done 'in a way which is meaningful to students, parents and employers, and therefore, above all simple, and without prejudice to A level standards' (MacGregor, 1990). From the vocational point of view, though General NVQs at Level 3 are intended to be the equivalent of A levels, core skill units are to be set up separately, but assessed during the performance of tasks in the vocational units.

Thus, the different bodies involved in the development of core skills post-16 have developed varying ideas about how they might be implemented. As subject-based courses, the emphasis in A Levels has been on the extent to which the core skills can be incorporated within syllabuses, without distortion. Both SEAC (SEAC, 1990b) and the NCC (NCC, 1990b) agree that of the six skills, communication, problem-solving and personal skills are capable of being applied to all A and AS syllabuses. However, they argue that numeracy, information technology and modern language competence cannot be embedded in all syllabuses in the same way. While all syllabuses may offer opportunity for using information technology to communicate information, not all subjects could easily incorporate simulations or modelling into their requirements. There was also a particular problem with modern language competence, where, because of the difficulties of incorporating it into subject provision, it was argued that students should have access to additional studies of foreign languages as part of their entitlement.

The NCVQ, on the other hand, has adopted a different approach to implementation. Whilst recognizing that competence in modern foreign languages is a special case, it has developed the idea of the other five core skills being specified as NVQ units in the same way that general vocational units are described. However, the evidence for core skill achievement will then come from the activities required to fulfil the requirements of the general vocational units and not through separate assessments. One additional refinement will be the division of personal skills into two types, one emphasizing individual performance and the other focusing on working with others (NCVQ, 1991).

Two further difficulties have been identified in relation to the implementation of core skills post-16. First, there is the danger that core skills might become part of the 'phantom curriculum'. That is, because they are no one's specific responsibility, they will become an area of neglect rather than of progress (Stanton, 1990a). Secondly, the incorporation of core skills into Advanced Level provision may imply some restriction on subject choice, unless there are additional opportunities to pursue a core skill in individual programmes of study (Boffy, 1990a). Thus, there is likely to be an increased need for opportunities for individual students to negotiate with tutors, or seek guidance and tutorial support in order to achieve appropriate levels of attainment in core skills.

What little evidence exists about the implementation of core skills tends to highlight the division between vocational and academic approaches. For example, it has been found that BTEC courses in FE Colleges tend to have the most advanced development in the area of core skills, while a coherent provision of core skills in Advanced Level courses has proved difficult because of the wide range of combinations of courses which 'academic' students follow (HMI, 1990a). Analyses of specific Advanced Level subjects (Nettleship, 1990; Shelton, 1990; Wood, 1991) have tended to show how core skills are already delivered in many existing A Level programmes of study, though often in an implicit way. They have also emphasized how core skills can be enhanced through an explicit recognition of their importance and the development of teaching and learning styles in the post-16 sector. However, these reports also recognize the considerable change in assessment procedures which would follow on from the incorporation of core skills in all Advanced Level subjects.

Issues concerning core skills

There has been widespread support for core skills as a basis for post-16 curriculum provision from industry, the vocationalists and the academic institutions, with all the major interested 'baronies' being involved in the consultation process (Ruddiman, 1990). However, while there is surface unanimity, the two wings of the 'alliance' may have offered their support for different purposes and with different expected outcomes. Indeed, the participation of such a diverse range of agencies may have raised expectations for core skills which cannot be met and the continued delay by the interested groups in reporting on core skills suggests difficulties in reaching a consensus among them.

Because the vocational and academic groups are approaching the issue from different starting points, they may not necessarily end up in the same place, with the aim of bridging the gap between the two educational routes proving to be difficult if not impossible to meet. For example, the NCC defines the National Curriculum in terms of attainment targets *and* programmes of study, while the NCVQ relies on outcomes only. Vocational courses are not usually made up of separately examined 'subjects'; instead units are built up to count towards the final qualification. Therefore, units of core skills could be developed. With Advanced and AS Level, subjects are examined and certificated separately, so that a 'core skill unit' in numeracy for an A Level mathematics student would have little saliency or meaning. Therefore, core skills would have to be built into A Level syllabuses and not stand as separate units.

The notion of a bridge between academic and vocational routes may also be resisted by employers and the universities. Employers involved in shaping vocational education and training may see core skills as an unnecessary complication of their training programmes (TES, 1990a). The more generalist approach to Advanced Level study suggested by core skills is likely to provoke resistance from the specialists, who have often fought hard to retain their 'domains of knowledge' (MacFarlane, 1990). If academic qualifications are still given priority in selection by employers and the institutions of higher education, then the equivalence of the NVQ will be in theory only.

Another important issue concerns the nature of the core skills and their transferability. We have already noted that the six skills are seen by the 'academic' grouping as naturally falling into two categories, but the problematic nature of the definition of core skills extends further than this. For example, personal skills concern the styles of learning adopted by students, and yet there is no general agreement on how these may be identified and assessed. While NCVQ identifies 'taking responsibility' and 'working with others' as the central features of personal skills (NCVQ, 1991), these are open to subjective interpretation and definition. Similarly, the skill of problem-solving has caused a great deal of comment (Coates, 1991; Wolf, 1990) over whether techniques of solving problems in one area of the curriculum can be divorced from context and transferred to other areas. Whereas NCVQ tends to accept the notion of transferability, academic educationalists are much less likely to accept that the context of learning is unimportant.

Moreover, the brief given by the Secretary of State was explicit in stating that the introduction of core skills should not 'distort' Advanced Level syllabuses, and this echoes the concern of the SEAC subject committees (SEAC, 1990b). To avoid distortion, core skills are likely to remain defined in general terms and only applied to A Level syllabuses where this can be done in the context of the subject. This may have the effect of making core skill provision in A Level syllabuses explicit, but any individual's A Level programme will not then necessarily provide a common core with vocational qualifications.

Following from this, there are likely to be difficulties in assessing core skill attainment in any post-16 course. While NCVQ has opted for four levels of attainment in each core skill unit, it is still not clear how these levels are to be defined and how subjective judgements concerning, for example, the personal skills of a student can be standardized across the different contexts for the purposes of assessment (Wolf, 1990). The notion that core skills cannot be assessed separately from the context in which they are exercised creates problems for the notion of credit transfer. If skills acquired in one context (an occupational unit) are to be credited to another context (an A Level), then the candidate will have shown competence in the skill, but not in the context for which she or he is being credited (Coates, 1991).

Other concerns which have been raised by the idea of core skills are:

- whether core skills can provide the framework for continuity from the National Curriculum (NCC, 1990a);
- whether core skills can provide the breadth and balance deemed necessary (FEU, 1990);
- whether core skills will lead to curriculum overload for post-16 students (Low, 1990);
- where the resources and staff to implement them will be found (Education, 1990).

Conclusion

While the aim of core skills post-16 may be to bridge the vocational-academic divide, it is far from clear that this will be the outcome. While there are formidable technical difficulties in defining and assessing core skills, there are also powerful political and cultural forces which are likely to reduce the impact of core skill reform on the post-16 curriculum. By insisting on the integrity of the 'gold standard' of A Levels, the Government has handed a strong case to those thinkers on the right who would see a return to traditional educational discourses (Jones, 1989). On the left, there remains a scepticism that any initiative which ignores the differentiation within society can only be tinkering with the system (Avis, 1990).

Also, the notion of the A Level as a 'gold standard' is deeply ingrained in the culture of British society and in the practices of employers and university admissions officers. As Coates (1990) has suggested, the likely outcome of the introduction of core skills would be some minor modifications of A Level syllabuses, which would do little to bridge the academic-vocational divide. Therefore, to see core skills as the solution to this division between the academic and vocational routes may be to pin too much hope on a single initiative, which is therefore bound to disappoint both sides of the 'alliance' who have put so much effort into making core skills a reality.

CHAPTER 8

Training and Enterprise Councils
Malcolm Maguire

The creation of the Training and Enterprise Councils (TECs) in England
and Wales and Local Enterprise Companies (LECs) in Scotland has
been, arguably, the most significant government policy innovation relating to the system of vocational education and training (VET) in Britain
in the last two decades. The prime purpose in the establishment of the
TECs has been to introduce a demand-led system, wherein those most
directly confronted with the deficiencies and requirements of the workplace – the employers – are given overriding responsibility for the determination of training provision. This in itself has significant implications
for the 16–19 age group. Moreover, as will be shown later, TECs have
also taken over responsibility for measures which are specifically targeted on that age group. It will also be seen that a number of areas of concern, in respect of the TECs' ability and suitability to achieve their ulti-
mate goal of eliminating the acknowledged deficiencies in the nation's
skills base, remain unresolved.

The emergence of TECs

The idea for the TECs was derived from the Private Industry Councils
(PICs) in the USA, although, as is often the case with policy-borrowing,
little attention seems to have been paid to establishing whether they were
operating successfully. Ewart Keep asserts that the decision to introduce
TECs,

> was ultimately taken, not as the result of any detailed academic research or evalu-
> ation of PICs, but rather as a consequence of a study tour of a representative sam-
> ple of two PICs by the then-current Secretary of State for Employment (Ryan,
> 1991, p.25).

As a result of that visit Cay Stratton, who had been involved in the PICs
in Massachussetts, was brought over by the Department of Employment

to act as a consultant during the implementation of the TEC initiative. As Maclure (1991b, p.16) points out, it is curious that a policy initiative should have been borrowed from the United States, where criticisms of the training system in comparison to those of Japan and Germany are widespread, as is the case in Britain.

The proposals for the TECs in England and Wales emerged in the White Paper *Employment for the 1990s* (DE, 1988). They were launched in March 1989 with a remit which included taking over responsibility for local delivery of the Government's enterprise and training programmes (including YTS), identifying, through research, local labour market needs, liaising with all local bodies concerned with enterprise, encouraging more private sector investment in training initiatives, and generating a shift from a supply-led to a demand-led training system. Eighty-two individual TECs have begun operations in England and Wales, each with a Board consisting of up to 15 members, two thirds of whom should be drawn from local industry and commerce, with the remainder customarily being representatives of local authorities, trade unions and voluntary organizations.

The Training Agency's publication *Training and Enterprise Councils: A Prospectus for the 1990s*, set out five 'principles for reform' which would form the basis for the launch of the TECs. Briefly stated, these were that:

- they would be employer-led, thereby transferring responsibility for the national training system from the public sector to the private sector;
- being locally based they would enable the training system to be tailored to local labour market needs;
- their responsibilities would encompass the areas of training, enterprise and vocational education, thereby creating greater coordination between programmes in these different areas;
- there would be an 'accent on performance', with a greater emphasis on cost-effectiveness than had previously been the case;
- they were to be 'born of the enterprise culture, with a bold vision that stretches beyond existing programmes, institutions and traditional methods of delivery'.

Their intended target groups were: employers, who would be encouraged to undertake more training; young people leaving full-time education; the long-term unemployed; the education system in terms of enhancing its relevance to the world of work; and small firms and the self-employed. On becoming operational they would take over responsibility for existing Government programmes such as Employment Training (ET), YTS (now YT), Business Growth Training (BGT) and the Enterprise Allowance Scheme. More recently they have been charged with responsibility for the Department of Employment's spending on Work-related Further Education, for the piloting of Training Credits, for sponsorship of Education-Business Partnerships including Compacts and have been given a role in helping to oversee TVEI.

Clearly, then, TECs will exert a powerful influence, not only on the training opportunities available to 16–19 year olds, but also on broader labour market issues, particularly in relation to local labour markets. However, before assessing the likely immediate impact on young people's opportunities, it is necessary to look more closely at the fundamental rationale for their introduction.

The rationale for TECs examined

TECs were born out of the acceptance of the fact that, in order to compete internationally, Britain needed to redress the deficiencies in its workforce, which was acknowledged to be insufficiently skilled. The two fundamental tenets of TECs are, first, that they hand over responsibility for training to employers, and second, that they enable training provision to become more responsive to local labour market needs. From the outset, indeed long before any of the TECs became operational, questions were raised about the wisdom of this approach.

In terms of the TECs being employer-led, more than a few eyebrows were raised at this prospect, as the conventional wisdom was that one of the main reasons for Britain's perceived backwardness in its provision of training, in comparison to our international competitors, was the marked reluctance of employers generally to participate in the training of their employees. Also, much of the rhetoric directed at the education system during the 1980s effectively berated it for failing to provide what employers want, thereby taking it for granted that employers have very clear ideas of what their short-, medium- and long-term manpower and training needs will be. This is highly questionable to say the least, even at a time of economic buoyancy. Writing at a time when Britain is enduring its most protracted recession since the Second World War, the notion becomes completely untenable.

This scepticism concerning the efficacy of transferring responsibility for overseeing training provision to an employer-led body needs to be qualified on two counts. First, recent research (Rainbird and Maguire, 1991) has suggested that, since the mid-1980s, there has been a significant shift in employers' attitudes towards training, with the value placed on training being considerably increased and often acknowledged at the highest levels within organizations. Unfortunately, these studies were undertaken prior to the onset of the current recession and therefore the permanence and stability of this shift is questionable in the absence of further investigation.

Second, it has always been the case, in all labour markets, that a relatively small core of employers, often comprising predominantly large organizations, have evinced a strong commitment towards training. Therefore, the generalization that employers have not previously been willing to undertake responsibility for the training of the national workforce has only been partly true. However, this in itself throws up another serious question mark about the long-term viability of the TECs. One of the reasons for making them employer-led was that this would encourage many small and medium-sized companies, who had previously shown no great willingness, to participate in training. It was believed that they would be more likely to become involved if the initiative was in the hands of fellow employers, rather than government agencies or other bodies associated with officialdom. This notion seems overly optimistic. Earlier research carried out by the Centre for Labour Market Studies in five different localities in Britain found that employers exhibited a marked reluctance to become involved in locally-based VET initiatives (Ashton *et al.*, 1989). Similarly, a study undertaken by the Centre for Corporate Strategy and Change at the University of Warwick, as part of the 'Training in Britain' study, found little evidence of employers attempting to influence the existing training system.

The distinction between large firms and small to medium-sized firms in their attitudes towards involvement in training is an important one, and was acknowledged when the TECs were being set up, by the stipulation that the employer representatives on TEC boards should be drawn from both large and small firms. A slightly different perspective on the concern over the possible domination of the TECs by representatives of large firms emerged from work by Prais, Jarvis and Wagner, who suggested that,

> it will be important to ensure that...(TECs)...do not become dominated by large firms, with their greater scope for personnel trained in narrow specialisations, and that the needs of smaller establishments for broadly-trained personnel are adequately represented (Ryan, 1991, p.140).

An additional point to be made about the future participation of the mass of employers in training is that, under present policies, it is being left to the powers of exhortation rather than to compulsion. Although it is still, clearly, too early to say whether the desired changes in attitude are being effected, the signs are not propitious.

The second major underlying principle of the TECs, namely that training provision should become more closely tailored and relevant to local labour market needs, appears, at one level, to be less contentious. Research has shown that for many young people their life chances are greatly influenced by the characteristics of the local labour market (Ashton and Maguire, 1986). The structure of job opportunities in a local area, being a function of the local industry mix and level of economic buoyancy, effectively determines not only young people's access to jobs, but also their subsequent opportunities for job movement, the availability of training provision, and, crucially, individuals' attitudes towards work and training. It is therefore desirable that the training system should be made more responsive to the requirements of individual local labour markets.

However, the focus on local labour markets can also be deemed to be questionable when considered in the light of how the labour market, and especially the youth labour market, operates. At the lower levels of the occupational hierarchy both job-seekers and recruiters restrict their search to the local area. Thus, when recruiting for semi-skilled and unskilled manual jobs and for routine clerical jobs, employers would customarily advertise in the local area, or use less formal word-of-mouth methods of recruitment. Similarly, job-seekers who are focusing on these types of jobs would normally look at the local press or other localized sources of job vacancy information. In contrast, at the upper levels, incorporating, for example, professional, managerial and technical jobs for which high levels of academic qualifications are almost always required, both recruitment and job-seeking would be more likely to be conducted on a national, or at least a regional basis. Thus, the higher one moves up the occupational hierarchy, the less significant becomes the TEC, as a body which is confined to operating in a local area. An implication of this may be that TECs become synonymous with the provision of lower-level skills training. If this should happen at a time when occupational shifts are rapidly reducing the number of workers required at these lower levels and when it is acknowledged that, as a nation, Britain has an increasing need for intermediate and higher-level skills and qualifications, then it is questionable whether TECs can be said to be addressing the issue of the long-term needs of a competitive economy.

Another drawback of TECs being locally orientated is that, as Coffield (1990, p.71) states, 'their programmes are designed to be local and tactical', and this is likely to detract from the effectiveness of any planning carried out at a national level. Although these dangers may be exaggerated given that approximately 80 per cent of TECs' spending is 'spoken for' by existing government programmes such as ET and YT, the thought of 82 TECs in England and Wales alone operating with a degree of autonomy does not bode well for future attempts to impose some order and strategic thinking into the national training system.

The 'local and tactical' element of TECs may also result in their being more concerned with what they have identified as the short-term needs of particular local industries without sufficient regard for what is in the best interests of individual trainees.

Counterbalancing these worries, it has been suggested that, in any case, the fact that the bulk of the funding for TECs is allocated at a national level will prevent their being regarded as truly local bodies.

Another problem facing the TECs has been what they perceive to be a potentially dangerous reduction in the level of Government funding being allocated. When this occurred in each of the first two years of operation, it led to TECs having to re-examine the targets which they had set, and to some of the leading industrialists participating in the development of TECs questioning the ability of TECs to provide the pervasive local administrative training role that had been envisaged for them. These difficulties created by reductions in funding have been exacerbated by the effects of rising levels of unemployment and the impact of the recession on companies. This has resulted in an increasing number of young people seeking places on YT, at the same time as adverse economic conditions mean that fewer companies are prepared to offer YT places. This is severely undermining the ability of TECs to fulfil the Government's guarantee of a place being available for all young people who seek one. It was feared that the lack of adequate funds would lead to a reduction in the budget per trainee of up to 8 per cent in 1992/93 (*The Guardian*, 22 January 1992, p.6).

Notwithstanding the aforementioned reservations, misgivings and foreseeable problems related to the introduction of TECs, they are likely to be with us, either in their present form or with adaptations, for some years to come. As such they will impact on the education and training of 16–19-year-olds in a number of ways. The first concerns their responsibility for YT, which is a development of the Youth Training Scheme (YTS). When it was first introduced, YTS was very successful in establishing a national scheme over a very short period of time. In 1985 it catered for 45 per cent of 16-year-old school-leavers and a growing proportion of 17-year-olds. Moreover, it provided young people with an alternative to unemployment which was generally welcomed. It also succeeded in reinforcing the notion that young people are entitled to a period of training when they first enter the labour market.

Despite these achievements YTS, and subsequently YT, have been beset by difficulties. It should be noted here that while YTS/YT will be referred to in general terms as a single scheme, it is acknowledged that there have been regular changes in the make-up of the programme, which began as a one-year voluntary scheme before becoming a two-year scheme which was virtually compulsory for the unemployed, and subsequently emerging as Youth Training, with different objectives.

One of the main problems faced by YTS, which is now re-surfacing to confront YT, was that it was expected to perform the dual function of providing training and alleviating unemployment. This identification with the unemployed created an image of low-level training as a substitute for 'real' jobs which was never wholly deserved but which has become difficult to shift.

As a training scheme it has been criticized in terms of the fact that fewer than half the trainees secured recognized qualifications, and even then only at a low level, and that the training provided failed to meet the demands of the local labour market (Turbin, 1987). Between April 1990 and March 1991 the proportion of YT trainees gaining a qualification had fallen to 38 per cent, from 43 per cent the year previously (Unemployment Unit and Youthaid, 1992). Also, unemployment among those leaving YT rose from 14 per cent to 20 per cent. The objectives of the new YT acknowledge these previous deficiencies in that they now aim for a minimum attainment level of NVQ Level 2 and place the emphasis on higher-level skills. However, the availability of YTS places has clearly been susceptible to change, dependent on the level of economic buoyancy. In the mid- to late-1980s, at a time of economic upturn and declining unemployment, many employers, notably in the South East, who were competing for scarce labour, pulled out of YTS and recruited school-leavers directly into jobs where they did not have to meet even the minimal training requirements of YTS. Thus, the relationship between participation in YT and youth unemployment has been maintained. It remains to be seen whether the exhortations of employer-led TECs will lead to a significant increase in the number of work placements being offered by employers.

TECs' responsibilities will also impinge on 16–19-year-olds through their role as managers of the training credits scheme, by which school-leavers will receive a two-year entitlement to training.

The objectives of each scheme are to increase the motivation of young people to continue with quality training and vocational education when they join the labour market, as well as to increase the numbers of young people in training and the levels of their qualifications (Michael Howard, Secretary of State for Employment, August 30, 1990,

102

The consequences of these schemes are as yet unclear, although it is hoped that they will enhance the value of training and education in the eyes of young people and encourage employers to seek to attract the best school-leavers by offering the opportunity for high quality training, whether it be provided by colleges of further education, private training providers or others. Although it may be argued that the most beneficial effects of the introduction of training credits are likely to be in terms of helping to change attitudes towards training by reinforcing the message that greater participation in training benefits both the employer and the individual trainee, it will require considerable support from TECs to achieve this. TECs will have a key strategic role to play in the implementation of the scheme, not least in determining the cash value of the credits and the training provision which they are able to purchase.

The introduction of training credits has implications for the funding mechanism of colleges of further education, by effectively transferring some of the responsibility from LEAs to TECs. In addition, by being given responsibility for that part of the work-related further education budget which was previously administered by the Employment Department, TECs have been handed a degree of influence over further education as a whole. The aim here is to ensure that FE provision becomes more responsive to the needs of the local labour market. TECs will exert considerable influence over the planning of work-related further education provision.

Conclusion

The implementation of a demand-led or employer-led strategy for determining vocational and educational training provision, such as that represented by the introduction of TECs, undoubtedly has some attractions. By locating the decision-making process at the local level, it hands over influence and responsibility to locally-based employers who are recruiting the products of the VET system and who, in theory at least, are in the best position to identify their needs.

The problem with this strategy is not that it brings the decision-making process to the local level, for that has been widely seen as a step forward for certain occupational levels. Rather, the problem lies in the assumption that, where training is concerned, employers' interests are equivalent to the national interest. As has been shown, employers in Britain are notoriously uneven in their commitment to training, with many undertaking little or no training. Few have any long-term, coordinated skill-supply strategy, and what training does take place is usually determined by the short-term needs of the company. Even among those who do train, the motivation for training take-up may not be synonymous with the upgrading of the skills of the workforce. Training may be provided in order to enhance workers' commitment to the organization, or as a tool for communicating company policy/culture to the workforce. Therefore, by placing employers in control of the TECs, there is no guarantee that their attitude to training will suddenly change and result in their adopting a longer-term perspective.

Indeed, recent research has highlighted the fact that employers are contributing to the failure of the educational system by attracting a high proportion of 16-year-olds into the labour market, often into dead-end jobs, by failing to recognize vocational qualifications, by failing to encourage the low-skilled to take up additional training, and by financially rewarding the decision to leave education (Ashton *et al.*, 1990). In view of all this, there can be little confidence in the expectation that employers alone can provide the appropriate means to bring about change in the VET system.

CHAPTER 9

TVEI - Change Through Categorical Funding

Derek D'Hooghe

TVEI, described as the most significant curriculum initiative in secondary education since Circular 10/65 (Dancy, 1984), was the first large-scale national intervention in the curriculum of English (and Welsh) schools. A key feature of the introduction of TVEI was the adoption of a new approach to change by which the central government used control of funding in an attempt to reconcile its desire to promote educational change with the strong traditions of local autonomy in curricula matters. It emerged through the MSC as the DES had no statutory power to provide the necessary financial resources nor, probably, would it have been sympathetic to its apparently vocational objectives. This approach has been designated as 'categorical funding' (Harland, 1987) and subsequently has been adopted in a number of MSC-directed work-related initiatives.

The main features of this strategy involve a central government agency allocating a fixed sum of money for an activity which it defines by a set of broad criteria announced in advance. The agency invites local authorities or other bodies to bid for an allocation from these earmarked funds with schemes that have been designed in accordance with these stated criteria, but whose shape has been determined by local needs. Once the central agency accepts a bid, a contract is signed, specifying in some detail what will be done in return for the funds provided, and contract compliance is assured through a built-in system of formal monitoring. This chapter will examine the origins of TVEI, its background and method of introduction and will assess its influence on 16–19 education and training.

The origins of TVEI

A major initiative by the Manpower Services Commission in the maintained education sector was anticipated by DES officials as early as 1981

(D'Hooghe, 1984, p.19). Although it was not clear at the time what form the initiative might take, it emerged under the title of the (New) Technical and Vocational Education Initiative. It was announced by the then Prime Minister, Margaret Thatcher, on 12 November 1982 after a meeting with the Chairman of the MSC, David Young. The MSC was then approaching the peak of its national influence over education and training policy.

The initiative was launched with no consultation with the education establishment and immediately met substantial opposition from teacher unions and many LEAs. Fears were expressed primarily about the threat to the 'liberal education (which) makes the gentleman' described by Cardinal Newman in the 1850s and which so continues to dominate education policy (Barnett, 1986, p.213). When the national criteria for submissions were published, the education establishment was appeased by the fact that bids would only be accepted through LEAs. The MSC requirement that a distinctive TVEI cohort be identifed for monitoring purposes created significant further opposition. There was also widespread concern that funding, equivalent to a doubling of the unit of expenditure, was being concentrated in a limited number of institutions and, within them, on a small target group. This requirement for a limited cohort of TVEI students which it was hoped would enable comparative studies to be made, had the benefits of a targeted approach but eventually proved to be a major obstacle to whole-institutional change. The expansion of the initiative also caught observers by surprise. Even before the first students embarked on their TVEI programmes in September 1983, the government announced that further pilot schemes would be launched the following year, 1984, a timescale for development that was to be repeated with subsequent phases of the project. Such was the influence of the MSC in 1986 that they were able to announce the extension of the initiative to all students in the 14–19 age range. All LEAs were invited to make bids to meet the extension criteria but the funding at a total cost approaching £1000m (DE/DES, 1986) was significantly less per pupil than in the pilot phase.

The introduction of TVEI was intended to test ways of organizing, managing and resourcing replicable programmes of technical and vocational education for 14–18-year-old people across the ability range. It reflected concern about the state of technical and vocational education, the apparent failure of the system to prepare young people for adult and working life as well as a perceived need to increase participation rates post-16. The national criteria for projects reflected the following concerns: a requirement for a four-year curriculum with progression from year to year; curriculum balance between general, technical and vocational elements; the development of initiative, enterprise and problem-solving skills; equality of opportunity; planned work experience; good careers and educational counselling and regular assessment.

At a time when schools were feeling the effects of cuts in public expenditure, the offer of a very sizeable injection of funding proved to be very attractive and the majority of LEAs prior to extension put in bids to meet the criteria. But the debate in many schools, both those choosing to participate and those rejecting it, continued unabated. In the early TVEI pilots many school bids had been formulated by a few senior managers with little opportunity for consultation with staff in the time allowed between the publishing of the criteria, notification of bids and the start of the projects.

LEA, school and college staff provided competitive bids within a few weeks, often with little previous experience of working in this way. Collaboration between staff in different institutions increased immediately as various models for cooperation emerged. Indeed, Bradford LEA completed a major building scheme linking their two project schools during the summer holidays in 1983 within weeks of receiving initial approval of their bid.

The high level of targeting on a few LEAs, schools, students and curriculum areas created further opposition but it did provide sufficiently concentrated resourcing to create some radical proposals. Had these problems been avoided by a more even distribution of resources, it is unlikely that observable change would have occurred and the necessary political support would not have been sustained.

It was soon clear that for virtually all the staff directly involved the national criteria provided a liberation from resource constraints and conventional expectations, but early evaluations pointed to the existence of 'innovation enclaves' (Saunders, 1985) in schools and colleges with few using the opportunity provided by TVEI 'to review and reshape the whole 14–18 curriculum' (Barnes et al., 1987).

Changes of focus in TVEI

TVEI was initially seen simply as a vehicle for curriculum change. The first proposals tended to focus on new courses in schools or in off-site centres. The courses were mainly of a technological or pre-vocational flavour, usually isolated from other areas of the curriculum and generally for a limited proportion of the week. Emphasis in the early projects was particularly on information technology (IT), links with industry and technology which did not then even feature as an 'area of experience' in

HMI's analysis of the curriculum (HMI, 1977). In 1982, there was virtually no IT activity in schools outside the limited provision of computer studies courses for O and A Level students which had emerged during the 1970s. Science, technology and careers staff emerged as the principal beneficiaries of the increased resources. Teachers of the humanities, arts and modern languages looked on with increasing concern as this additional support went elsewhere and into innovative schemes which often eroded their own time allocation in the curriculum.

After the initial phase of project development as a result of which technology and IT gained an accepted place in the curriculum, more emphasis was placed on changing teaching and learning styles. Student-centred approaches were promoted with many schemes focusing on developing 'experiential', 'active' and problem-solving approaches. This led rapidly to proposals for new forms of assessment, particularly new GCE/CSE mode 3 syllabuses or existing courses accredited by CGLI or other vocational bodies. This legitimized the TVEI role in the whole curriculum and it led to a greater emphasis on staff development to bring about changes in teaching styles and to incorporate aspects of pre-vocational experiences and IT skill development across the curriculum. Thus the early fears of a narrow vocational curriculum were avoided in the later developments.

To reflect these initiatives, the nature and organization of staff development in schools and colleges also began to change, moving from a model based predominantly on secondments to award-bearing courses in institutions of higher education or courses organized by advisers, to one involving groups of staff working together with external support. In response to the opportunities provided by funding from TVEI Related In-Service Training (TRIST) and the recognition that curriculum and staff development were inextricably linked, staff development became more institution-focused. As the release of teachers from classes, covered by supply staff, became increasingly disruptive, TVEI projects explored the use of residential weekend courses or additional payments for evening courses.

It also became apparent that organizational development was the third important area through which TVEI could achieve its objectives. Schools and colleges appointed a TVEI Coordinator, generally at a head of department level (senior lecturer in FE) in the pilot, although increasingly a deputy head in the extension. In the early stages, TVEI Coordinators and their teams were not always effectively integrated into the existing organizational structures, thereby making it difficult to manage change. As TVEI and other curriculum initiatives developed in the 1980s, a new role of 'Coordinator' emerged. Members of staff received responsibility allowances for areas such as IT across the curriculum, equal opportunities and CPVE. This group, often sponsored and funded by TVEI, had a greater whole-institution perspective than conventional heads of department. They also had access to resources to create change which were of an order undreamed of by other senior staff. But they still did not fit easily into the conventional organizational structure, often being excluded from the senior management team or such groups as heads of department.

Successful developments depended on the recognition by senior managers of the interdependence of curriculum, staff and organizational development. Geoff Stanton, Chief Officer of the Further Education Unit, believed that TVEI was the first large-scale educational project to recognize and support this approach (FEU, 1989b, p.5; Stanton, 1990b). This interdependence of curriculum, staff and organization development was soon perceived as being equally relevant to the operation of LEAs, particularly to their Advisory Services. In many LEAs, TVEI had been seen as an isolated curriculum project with a Coordinator appointed at headship level within, or linked to, the existing Advisory Service. Where the Chief Adviser or other senior member of the LEA played a prominent role in TVEI, acting as a patron to the Coordinator, the project was able to engage advisers on a relatively broad front. More often, TVEI paddled its own canoe and frequently found difficulty in engaging mainstream advisory staff who shared many of the reservations expressed by school staff. Indeed, many felt challenged by the principles, style and terminology of TVEI. As the TVEI extension has developed in LEAs, it has increasingly raised questions about organizational structures, roles and accountability which have not been easily resolved.

Another important organizational aspect of TVEI for both institutions and LEAs has been the emphasis on collaboration. Groups of schools and colleges have been expected to work closely within LEAs and have frequently been responsible for developing joint proposals and deploying substantial resources. Heads have often worked closely together despite the frequent strains and, more recently, the expectation of competition promoted by the 1988 Education Reform Act. Teachers and lecturers across schools and FE colleges have worked jointly on curriculum and staff development to support new programmes of study both pre- and post-16.

This has been equally true at the LEA level where LEA staff worked together in their pilot phase or, as TVEI embraced more authorities, on a regional basis. Joint LEA projects were encouraged by the MSC not only in TVEI itself but subsequently in TRIST, the Flexible Learning Initiative and other areas. Whilst LEAs and schools often felt that such complex collaborative working arrangements imposed on them for little financial benefit had enormous unaccounted staffing costs, the other gains have probably justified the model. It will be interesting to see how it evolves in the climate of LMS.

16–19 Initiatives

The challenges to curriculum developers working in 16–19 education have proved to be greater than those in pre-16 provision. Progress in the first eight years of TVEI has been only on the margins as the necessary wholesale reform has been inhibited, primarily by vested interests with powerful, national influence. The TVEI Unit has been thwarted in its bid to change the nature of the A Level curriculum by the strength of the 'gold standard' lobby. Equally, it has been frustrated by claims from within the FE sector that many of the changes promoted by TVEI were already being addressed as a result of pressure from vocational examining boards to make teaching, learning and assessment more active and student-centred in both pre-vocational and vocational courses.

At the LEA level, TVEI acted as a catalyst for many LEAs to produce for the first time statements of curriculum entitlement for the whole 16–19 age range typically based on principles, processes and outcomes of learning. More recently, central guidelines for TVEI extension in the 16–19 age range have set out specific focused areas for development including targets and performance indicators involving Records of Achievement, Individual Action Planning, Flexible Learning and work-related experiences. TVEI has thus attempted to influence both the structure and the learning processes of the 16–19 curriculum.

It has long been felt that the structure of the post-16 curriculum in England and Wales was in need of reform. Education provision for this age group has been characterized, relative to many of our economic competitors, by low participation rates, narrow specialization and a dual track of academic A Level courses in schools and vocational provision in FE. During the period of rising youth unemployment of the 1970s and 1980s the 'new sixth' expanded rapidly to cater for an increasing group (re)taking GCE O Level or studying pre-vocational programmes, particularly CPVE.

Numerous unsuccessful attempts have been made to change the structure of Advanced Level courses, most recently the Higginson report (DES, 1988) which was widely endorsed by schools, higher education and industry. Opposition from some parts of the independent schools sector and the Prime Minister's office was sufficient to block the proposals. The recommendation that there should be five leaner but still rigorous A Levels was rejected by the Government on the grounds that standards would be eroded (see Chapter 3).

One of the recommendations of the report relating to support for modularization was already being supported by TVEI. The early modular schemes included the Wessex and 5 Counties projects but there are now six well established modular schemes. These A Level syllabuses typically provide students with an opportunity to choose from a large number of modules to gain accreditation usually requiring six modules for an A Level and three for an AS. The schemes also provide opportunities for interim unit accreditation and the submission of course work, although the latter is not confined to modular schemes. Frequent claims are made for the success of modular schemes in improving students' motivation. The Associated Examining Board reported (*TES*, 24 May 1991) that the modular project had reduced the drop-out and failure rate from 30 per cent to 10 per cent, whilst 40 per cent of the first batch of exam candidates achieved A grades. Some of these modular A Level schemes are planned to facilitate dual accreditation with BTEC courses. However, this device to bridge the academic and vocational divide has become increasingly difficult as BTEC reforms in the late 1980s have encouraged the development of internal integration in their courses and the NCVQ has introduced a competence-based assessment system which is incompatible with A Levels in their present form.

Some success has been achieved with the use of CPVE as a curriculum framework for all post-16 provision in an institution (FEU, 1987). Whilst this has been primarily used to bring together one-year GCSE provision with the separate CPVE 'stream', in some schools it has embraced all students in their first year in the sixth form. This has provided an organizational structure to address the introduction of entitlement and core skills. This may be jeopardized, however, with recent changes to the CPVE structure.

Efforts to change the structure of the vocational curriculum have had variable success. There has been a real or perceived reluctance by the vocational accreditation bodies to develop dual accreditation to close the academic/vocational divide. Some FE colleges have taken advantage of TVEI funding to create link courses which have been particularly successful when jointly planned and offering opportunities for accreditation. Despite the progress made in some places through collaboration between schools and colleges, bringing together the academic and vocational curricula has been much easier in single institutions able to offer the entire range of post-16 courses. Substantial progress has been made in introducing a common core in FE, notably by the provision of improved arrangements for tutoring and guidance and counselling, which have been made easier by changes to the organizational structure of colleges. The promotion of a broad and balanced curriculum entitlement post-16 has come into conflict with the pressure from NCVQ to re-design courses to place more emphasis on the assessment of job-specific competence. However, FE colleges have found it difficult to apply the notion of entitlement to their provision for part-time students and have struggled to convince all employers of the value of a broader approach to education and training.

The difficulty of achieving major structural changes to post-16 curriculum and assessment has led TVEI projects to examine other means of creating change. These have focused on the learning and assessment processes within existing course structures as an integral part of the development of an entitlement curriculum for all 16–19-year-olds. In TVEI extension, the TVEI unit has provided guidance on the continuation of 14–16 developments including Records of Achievement, the use of Individual Action Plans, Flexible Learning and work-related activity.

TVEI has played a major part since the first round of pilot projects in the development of Records of Achievement. At times when the future of RoAs as anything more than a reporting device looked in doubt, TVEI has played a key role in supporting the use of RoAs as a key aspect of the entitlement curriculum with a contractual requirement that RoAs be an integral part of project submissions in the extension phase. The announcement of a National Record of Achievement (NRA) parallels the development work under the auspices of NCVQ of the National Record of Vocational Achievement (NRoVA).

The development of Records of Achievement has provided a significant focus for discussion with higher education institutions about changes in 14–19 education arising from TVEI. The growing interest shown by HE in TVEI developments has influenced the development of the Enterprise in Higher Education programmes and has begun to inform arrangements for admission into higher education. Such developments have not as yet proved powerful enough to enable schools to be sufficiently confident to rid themselves of the shackles of A Levels by introducing alternative forms of accreditation such as AS examinations, BTEC or the International Baccalaureat or a British equivalent (Finegold et. al., 1990).

TVEI has supported the move to integrate the process of action planning into the existing process of reflection and recording of previous achievement. This has involved extending the relationship between tutors and students by placing more emphasis on teachers and students meeting together on a planned and regular basis to identify mutually agreed targets for future action. The development of thinking about Individual Action Plans in TVEI owes much to the Youth Development Projects, the training credits pilot scheme and Compacts. Individual Action Planning is seen as playing an important contributory role in achieving the CBI target of 50 per cent of the employed workforce achieving NVQ Level 3, (CBI, 1991).

In the extension phase of TVEI, much emphasis has been placed on the promotion of Flexible Learning. Some ambitious targets have been set by TEED, notably to embed student-centred Flexible Learning into the curriculum of all 14–19-year-olds by 1993. The TVEI unit has funded three-year Flexible Learning development projects which have focused on three areas identified in a framework for the management of Flexible Learning (DE, 1991): managing teacher-student partnerships, managing the use of resources and managing teacher-student routes. Learning styles have begun to change in both A Level and BTEC provision. Supported self-study has been a favoured approach used within A level programmes, while in the vocational curriculum the preferred model has been the use of open-learning workshops.

The development of work-related activity has been extended in post-16 education as a result of TVEI. Work experience, work shadowing and industrial projects linked with mainstream studies have been introduced for the first time into the curriculum of many A Level students and these activities have been enhanced and extended in the vocational curriculum.

Conclusion

Has the TVEI strategy for achieving change in 16–19 education and training through the use of significant targeted resources been success-ful? The objectives of TVEI relate essentially to changes in the curriculum to equip young people for adult life and work. Whilst many changes have occurred in teaching practice, and ownership has been effectively transferred to teachers, the national constraints have prevented TVEI from achieving its full potential.

The process through which TVEI has influenced change in the 16–19 sector is complex. Much of this has been through informal influence with government departments and, for example, NCC, SEAC and NCVQ working groups. At the local level, LEAs have been required to put forward proposals for negotiation with the national TVEI unit. These have been incorporated either into the formal contract with the LEA or been part of the annual review process between (initially) the MSC and the LEA. The LEAs have in turn generally made 'contractual' arrangements with schools and colleges on which they have been expected to report annually. Where the MSC has not been satisfied by the quality of proposals or progress made, funding has been occasionally withheld from the LEA. The formal review process with the LEA has been augmented through 'inspections' involving TVEI staff examining classroom practice. More emphasis has been placed on schools and colleges monitoring and evaluating TVEI developments as part of their requirement to devise school and college development plans. In addition, a number of local and national evaluations, particularly by HE institutions, have been carried out. This relatively high level of contractual accountability through internal and external evaluation has had an important influence on change through a process of negotiation. The accountability has usually been felt by individual institutions. It has provided TVEI Coordinators in LEAs and schools with the ability to overcome much resistance, at least at the superficial level, by suggesting that funds may be lost if the contractual agreement is not fulfilled. This may find its way into the relationship between LEAs and the DES through GEST and other arrangements. It will almost certainly influence the Council for the 'independent' FE sector in the 1991 White Paper proposals for post-16 education and training (DES/DE, 1991a).

TVEI has been one of the most intensively evaluated curriculum development projects. Of the four items on the 'alliance' agenda referred to in Chapter 1, HMI inspections and national and local evaluations have shown that TVEI has had a strong and positive effect on teaching and learning. The initiative has demonstrated that a broader repertoire of teaching and learning styles can engage young people and increase and recognize a wider range of achievement. TVEI has also broadened the curriculum of A Level students by including work-related activities and IT. It has helped to elevate the status of vocational programmes and has promoted collaboration between schools and FE colleges.

As to the remainder of the agenda for reform there has been less success. Here the national strategy arguably has been inadequate in that the other issues have not been supported simultaneously by a coherent strategy with a national consensus. Research into the examination success of the cohort of students in TVEI pilot schemes was inconclusive (Fitz-Gibbon et al., 1988) and 'the early pilot projects were not successful in increasing participation in education and training' (HMI, 1991c). Indeed, there was so much national concern about the apparent lack of effect on post-16 participation rates that there was reluctance to release the information. The increase in achievement at 16 and the consequent rise in post-16 participation rates almost certainly owe more to the national introduction of GCSE (HMI, 1991c).

There are still large numbers of students for whom there is no satisfactory provision. The alternative tracks post-16 allow virtually no transfer; a quarter of the highest achievers fail A Level and leave with no credit; and the curriculum for individuals remains unduly narrow and an inadequate preparation for work in the 21st century. These remaining problems suggest that an incremental approach may be effective if it is within an overall strategy but if changes in interdependent areas are moving in mutually incompatible directions there may be no overall progress at all. In terms of organizational development, TVEI has had an influence on schools and FE colleges particularly through their Coordinators. It has also influenced approaches to evaluation through its promotion of the use of performance indicators which are now firmly on the national agenda. If the same level of resources had been delegated to schools and colleges without targeting, it is unlikely that the same level of change would have been achieved:

> Well targeted funding is an effective means of bringing about change. The process of inviting bids for funding, then screening and negotiating those bids, has been powerful in effecting change (HMI, 1991c).

TVEI demonstrates, above all, that changes to 16–19 education and training depend ultimately on a coherent expression of political will.

CHAPTER 10

The Necessity for Institutional Change

Michael Clegg

There seems now to be common agreement that Britain cannot compete
in the volume markets dominated by the emerging economies around the
Pacific rim and needs instead to compete in new high-technology and
high value-added markets. If the imperative to do this rests upon intellectual skills, then a source of significant worry is the system's inability to
provide any more than a comparatively small proportion of each age
cohort with a modicum of learning beyond the age of 16. In the race to
win markets for high-technology products, education has a key role to
play. A common provision of education and training up to the age of 18
was first seen as an aim as far back as 1917 when Fisher, in his report as
President of the Board of Education, made a proposal to provide compulsory day continuation classes for all young people from 14 to 18. Then,
as now, the proposals were seen as a

> far-seeing plan to fit the youth of the nation for the tremendous task they would have
> in rebuilding a country whose commerce had been shattered and whose wealth had
> been scattered by war (Lloyd George, 1936).

Most of his proposals regarding post-16 provision have lain dormant
ever since. More recently, but apparently equally doomed, the Manpower
Services Commission believed, almost 20 years ago, that one of its central roles would be to undertake a complete overhaul of Britain's education and training system.

It has been left to the post-16 education service, in all its forms, to
respond to the perceived need for increased participation and performance. Increased funding does not follow increased participation, as
many post-16 providers know only too well. Increased output, whether at
A Level or BTEC National Diploma, has increased the number of routes
open to school leavers at 18. Re-organizations of post-16 provision have
reflected the politically expressed aim of increased efficiency or economy. Nevertheless, in responding, the education service is reacting to

external pressure – the world market, higher technology and a realization that a successful economy requires an educationally successful work-force, almost as a *sine qua non*. Participation rates have increased significantly and proportions of young people achieving matriculation grades for entry into higher education have also increased. Pressure for places in higher education is running higher than ever.

There has been some debate nationally as to whether Britain can re-cast itself as a modern industrial nation either through incremental change or by a root-and-branch restructuring. The debate nationally will not be over for some years yet. However, it is the aim of this chapter to give some thought to the ways in which incremental change in our national system of education and training can exert pressure on the individual institution. Even incremental change nationally might mean root-and-branch change within one institution. New clients, new modes of learning, new funding mechanisms, even new legal identities, may all mean that a single institution could face massive reconsideration of its aims, and the manner of achieving those aims. It is possible to make incremental changes to systems and funding mechanisms, but, if any organization represents the sum of the working methods and attitudes of people within the structure, it is not so easy to make incremental changes to attitudes and perceptions.

Changes in post-16 provision

The first changes in post-16 provision were seen as achieving more efficient ways of providing for a comparatively small, expensive client group. Small school sixth forms were replaced in many areas by sixth form colleges, able to provide more subject choice, larger set sizes and thus lower unit costs. The increasing cost-effectiveness of the provision took advantage of concentrations of staff, mainly from school sixth form backgrounds, with high levels of expertise and commitment to their work. Forms of organization were very flat – the principal and a number of vice principals (most usually two or three), with an attendant large group of heads of department responsible for subject specialisms (for example, maths or languages). Few sixth form colleges opted for an extra tier of management at, say, faculty level. The absence of 11–16-year-olds increased the specialization of staff, whose subject expertise and teaching performance seemed to improve as a result. The quality of results achieved by the early sixth form colleges gave confidence to those considering a similar move.

The successes of the early sixth form colleges also encouraged a higher participation rate at 16+, so that larger numbers of students capable, or even only marginally capable, of A Level work continued with their studies and, in turn, a larger number of young people were able to apply for higher education. More sixth form colleges opened and the successes of the early colleges were repeated in later additions to the mode. The sixth form college has made a very positive contribution to the increased numbers of young people aiming for degree and higher diploma level work in universities and colleges.

As institutions, the sixth form colleges were not markedly different from their precursors, the larger sixth forms in schools. Staff carried similar responsibilities and the client group was only marginally different, but the colleges' ability to provide a post-16 experience divorced from the 11–16 school atmosphere was an undoubted attraction to young people. At the same time there was ample evidence (for those who looked) that the system of sixth form colleges had not diminished the quality of experience in partner 11–16 schools, either by the loss of teachers opting for sixth form teaching, or by the loss of the sixth form pupil as a role model. Indeed, there is evidence that the 11–16 schools, no longer needing to rob pupils in the first five years to pay for uneconomic sixth forms, were able to provide a better experience. The incremental change that saw the creation of sixth form colleges fed by a number of 11–16 schools resulted in a successful pattern of academic education for many young people.

The growth of the tertiary colleges

A second stage of incremental change soon became necessary, however, if sufficient opportunity were to be given to those young people for whom A Level work did not represent the automatic choice at age 16. Tertiary colleges provided a breadth of work which had previously been offered partly by sixth form study and partly by the kind of vocational education normally found in FE colleges. The emergence of tertiary colleges was seen as a step beyond the establishment of sixth form colleges. Many tertiary colleges were formed from mergers between sixth form colleges and FE colleges, but as institutions, they were different from both of their precursors. They were larger, frequently based on more than one site, and as a result of the Local Education Authority's approval for the formation of a college, they often had a specific responsibility to work closely with their partner comprehensive schools. They tended to have a more hierarchical organizational structure with more form to their' Articles of Government and, in contrast to the sixth form colleges, often acted as the providers of non-vocational evening work for adults.

Nevertheless, within the tertiary colleges, individual staff carried responsibilities comparable to those of their previous institutions. Lecturers in vocational areas and lecturers in general education were rarely expected to teach outside their given area of expertise, and in many 'phase one' tertiary colleges, a key objective was to ensure that the new college managed its new role without impairing any previous levels of expectation of performance.

The greatest changes derived from the tertiary colleges' ability to offer more to the individual student, and before long the 'phase two' tertiary colleges were re-examining their work to see if they could get away from rigid patterns of provision and offer courses to students which covered both A Level and vocational education elements. In fact, these courses have been very successful, both because students have valued the opportunity to delay choices which might otherwise have committed them to a wrong path too soon, and because the success rate in both elements has tended to be high. The following two paragraphs offer examples of the value of this approach.

Despite the success of GCSE examinations in encouraging a more positive learning style, not all students achieve the level of results necessary to allow them to progress to higher levels of work. Such students have been offered the painful opportunity to resit, with a five-subject GCSE programme typically including subjects which they have previously failed. Many students, not unexpectedly, are bored by this experience, and it is not surprising that the national success rate for GCSE resits should be as low as 20 per cent. In most tertiary colleges, however, students have the chance to combine two or three GCSE resits with a vocational education course at a similar level. The success rate for this provision is much higher: students tend to succeed in the GCSEs (after all, they choose the two or three in which they have the most chance of passing) and also gain a vocational qualification. A year of potential failure can be transformed into a year of achievement. A large percentage carry on at 17 to take a higher level vocational course, or an A Level course.

Other students in tertiary colleges benefit from the opportunity to take courses which cover A Level and vocational education elements. In schools and sixth form colleges there are many examples of young people who are offered the chance to drop one A Level 'to concentrate on the other two'. Success rarely follows this strategy, as the student often spends the extra time on the very activities that made a three-A Level programme such a trial. However, the chance to combine two A Levels with a vocational element often increases motivation, and certainly has much to offer the 18-year-old job hunter when approaching employers. This combination is now also providing a route into higher education at degree or higher national diploma level.

Teaching and learning styles in tertiary colleges tend to be more varied as students are often following programmes of study that cut across work which would previously have been regarded as needing different teaching and learning traditions. This variety has led to considerable development of teaching and learning styles in tertiary colleges through staff development programmes which draw on the best from these different traditions. The post-16 experience in a tertiary college is further divorced from the 11–16 school atmosphere and, again, this seems to be an undoubted attraction to young people. The tertiary colleges, along with their partner schools, have been successful in attracting a large proportion of school leavers into education and encouraging them to move through the education system to higher levels of attainment.

Root-and-branch change at the institutional level

Although the structural shift from sixth form provision in schools to the establishment of sixth form colleges and tertiary colleges was seen as change of an incremental kind, the type of change now being experienced within individual tertiary colleges is much more of the root-and-branch variety. The client groups attracted to tertiary colleges are undoubtedly from a wider background than those attending sixth form colleges. Those who come at age 16 have a much wider range of educational attainment and include those with intellectual or physical impairment which require special provision. In addition, adults and young people following day-release courses from employment form a significant feature of the tertiary colleges' clientele. Tertiary colleges are open in the evenings and for periods of the year when schools and sixth form colleges would be closed. Staff can expect to be involved with a wider range of student needs and to work with a different set of conditions of service, designed to increase flexibility.

As with sixth form colleges, tertiary colleges are expected to form close links with their partner comprehensive schools and to play an active role in shaping local arrangements for a school/college TVEI 14–19 curriculum. However, they are also required, through WRNAFE (Work-related Non-advanced Further Education) planning for example, to form links with other providers, especially the Training and Enterprise Councils.

Responding to the needs of different client groups has become something of an art-form in college management programmes. Each industry is setting its own targets, especially through the lead-body structure in the National Council for Vocational Qualifications. The CBI is setting national targets for participation and achievement. For the moment, the LEAs remain responsible for local planning of post-16 provision under the 1988 Education Reform Act. Central government, in spite of its keenness to set out a national curriculum for 5–16-year-olds, has so far given little meaningful direction at the post-16 level. Presumably, it can only be a matter of time before central government of one party or another sets out the stage and the only question is whether the change nationally will be root-and-branch or incremental.

In this rich mixture of change to institutions, to curriculum, to targets and to structures, colleges will need to redefine their methodologies. The key questions facing institutions are how they will accommodate to rapid change and how they will manage such a broad range of objectives. Many colleges already articulate their overall ambition through a 'mission statement', from which are derived more particular aims and objectives. The aims reflect the variety of challenges to the colleges and the need to set out the range of expectations which the governors of the colleges can look for in performance. Although there will be a variety of difficulties, a central problem exists if there is insufficient change in attitudes, especially among the existing senior managers, to reflect the developing aims and objectives of a college.

The change required of individuals will impact on their manner of working and this will, in turn, require for the institution a cultural change in expectations and styles of thought. Of course, bringing about change in attitudes is a key function of education itself. Why develop knowledge and understanding if it is not to bring about changes in how people think and perceive? But although colleges can be quite expert in producing this change in students, they forget to their peril that staff do not always receive the same opportunities for education.

Indeed, teachers or lecturers engaged in some areas of the work of colleges may find their day-to-day timetabled responsibilities quite similar over a period of years, whilst other colleagues are grappling with rapid change in the curriculum and the organization of teaching and learning. A good example would be the development of the BEC and TEC work into BTEC, and the development of NVQ. Teachers of A Level work were left almost untouched by this change at the time. The entire post-16 education world is waiting to see when, and in what form, the replacement of A Level will arrive!

In short, colleges may face the need for further development, for change in the culture of their working, which they have to address by a combination of means. Reorganization is one vehicle of cultural change; staff development is another. Opening new centres, either a small development department, or a new building separate from the parent body, has also been found a useful approach.

The biggest cultural changes are often brought about as secondary effects of changes in funding levels, for which the change in Youth Training provides a classic example. If reorganization is the most easily planned, most easily controlled and most easily measured method of bringing about change, then certain key steps emerge. It is imperative to establish key targets which have the very desirable effect of providing a clear picture of where an organization has to go.

Often not included in the range of considerations in any re-organization is the important element of communication, especially the extent to which a commitment is being made to good communications through a greater degree of pluralism in decision-making, a commitment, for example, to participative democracy. Colleges tend to see themselves as having a very flat hierarchical structure which lends itself to a 'senior common room' style of shared responsibility. This might not be enough if incorporation is visited upon colleges, especially with a much wider set of specialist responsibilities to manage.

In any case, it remains a mystery why so many colleges persist, particularly in the Further Education sector, in giving the responsibility for such wide strategic aims to heads of departments. They become responsible for marketing, admissions, curriculum, personnel, staff development, budgeting and other functions within their self-contained empires. It is questionable whether all heads of department have enough skills, or even enough of the wider college view, to manage the disparate range of objectives which colleges now face. If the college is serious about its objectives, the objectives might deserve specialist teams to carry them out.

Most colleges have a commitment to their communities and this is often referred to in their college mission statement. This commitment might be defined as extending to adults in the community, to employees in local firms and to school-leavers. Colleges set strategic aims for contacting, admitting and monitoring each of these client groups. Some colleges have procedures, often supported by BS5750 certification, for handling these interests. So far as a hierarchy of objectives is concerned, most colleges work admirably from a mission statement to quite detailed procedural objectives in an orderly and logical, well thought-out, manner. In too few cases, however, does a college's organizational structure present the same careful logic. The system on the ground can often be confusing and competitive between departmental interests on the one hand and student interests on the other. Do all departments follow the objectives in the same way? Do they have the same priorities between strategic objectives? Are all heads of department and their senior managers equally competent to manage student affairs, along with capital replacement programmes, curriculum innovation and timetabling?

Colleges will need, in the next few years of rapid change, to identify specialist teams of staff to manage more narrowly-focused strategic objectives, if the highest levels of management performance are to be achieved. Such teams might include, for example, a curriculum management team, with further sub-teams for curriculum innovation and management in specialist areas of the college like engineering or management studies. These teams could call on the specialist support of the staff development officer and the examinations officer, who may in turn each have their own team. There may be a student affairs team, supported by a specialist adult students team, a school-leaver team, an employed student team, and so on.

Specialist teams can have targets (participation rates from identified schools and successful completions by course are two examples) which can inform their progress. Specialist aspects of these targets can even be visited upon individuals. Indeed, in a world rapidly moving to performance-related pay, a more consistent and focused set of objectives provides a platform for higher standards which can be met with higher levels of remuneration.

How appropriate will the institution be to the needs of those forming the additional quartile of those staying on after age 16? Colleges cannot afford to reduce their concern for the needs of those already staying on and the advances made in quality, care and success must not be jeopardized. But it cannot be assumed that the next 25 per cent of school-leavers participating in post-16 education in colleges will necessarily look for the same experience as their peers already choosing post-16 education. They may prefer learning experiences different from spending longish periods of time in classes, with expectations of performance based so heavily on the written word. The experience of Youth Training has improved markedly over the last few years, but a much to be hoped for increase in the levels of NVQs might leave YT providers struggling. For this need, colleges will need to find the flexibility to provide training workshop programmes, good quality science and materials technology teaching, with drop-in centre support for basic educational needs such as literacy or numeracy. In other areas of the training curriculum, similar flexibility will need to be shown.

To manage the range of issues presenting themselves, colleges will certainly need some quality assurance system, either BS5750 or TQM.

Managing staff through this change will be crucial. However, if education is about encouraging an ability to change, colleges will need to bring about this development in their own staff.

Colleges will undoubtedly respond to the changes looming in the wings. Structure, aims and methodologies of management are important, but the overriding factor will be the extent to which colleges believe in themselves and in the value of their role in the development of our economy.

PART 3

The Progress of Change

CHAPTER 11

Significant Change or Lost Opportunity?
Louise Kidd

In the last decade, the opportunities and pressure for significant change in 16–19 education and training have been numerous. While some change, sponsored and approved by the Government, has taken place much has not due to the fact that education policies based on sound principles have taken second place to education politics rooted in an élitist system for the few. During the 1980s three key national players have formed an alliance for reform which has exerted much pressure and has influenced the national debate.

The MSC in *A New Training Initiative* (DE, 1981) put forward a strategic plan for education and training and sought to overhaul and rationalize the vocational education and training system. The TVEI programme exerted pressure through Government funding to vocationalize the curriculum 14–19. As the MSC became the TA and later TEED, TVEI funding and planning passed through the 14–16 phase and into the 16–19 phase. In the extension phase, the priority areas for development were promoting Flexible Learning and Records of Achievement, making students more aware of opportunities in industry by emphasizing the vocational dimension in an experience of work and improving local coordination of education/industry links. There was also a strong movement towards modular A/AS provision as a means of accrediting courses by assessment at a variety of stages.

The CBI (1989) in *Towards a Skills Revolution* outlined the need for common learning outcomes for 16–19-year-olds and for targets to bridge the skills gap. They further emphasized the need for a National Record of Achievement and Individual Action Plans and proposed a system of training credits for 16–19-year-olds.

The FEU through publications such as *A Basis for Choice* (FEU, 1979) were influential in promoting pre-vocational education. They put much emphasis on an entitlement curriculum for 16–19-year-olds, stressing the processes of learning as well as raising awareness of the value of vocational contexts in learning.

By the late 1980s not only was there significant pressure to realize the potential of vocational qualification but there was also apparent agreement on the need for breadth in all 16–19 education and training in the form of skills and competences. The CBI, NCC, NCVQ and SEAC virtually agreed on the six core skills which should be an integral part of all post-16 study programmes and that progress and attainment levels in these skills should be recorded in a Record of Achievement.

By the end of the 1980s there was a growing consensus that the A Level curriculum was in need of reform with some suggestion that change would be supported by the Government. Despite their rejection of Higginson, the Government asked SEAC in 1989 to review the principles governing A/AS examinations. However, by the time SEAC reported in November 1990, there had been a significant retrenchment by the Government in its stance to 'protect' the Advanced Level system from reform. As well as the strength of the academic tradition, other obstacles to reform were clearly identified in the 1980s. There was no history of a training culture in British industry and there was little established quality vocational education with employers still preferring either narrow job-specific training or academic qualifications rather than vocational qualifications even at low levels of attainment. It was clear at the start of the 1990s that the absence of a coherent and comprehensive plan for education, training and employment post-16 was disadvantaging this country. Fewer young people were continuing in education in Britain than in any other developed country (see Table 11.1).

These statistics were the catalyst that brought all parties to realize that coordination and planning at a national level were needed if Britain were to compete economically with other nations. Now as the end of the century approaches, one aim which unites politicians, the education profession and industry is that of increasing participation rates in education beyond compulsory school age and to raise standards of attainment.

Common targets, which are acknowledged to be very ambitious, have been agreed by the Government, industry and the other political parties. All have subscribed to the CBI target of 50 per cent of 16–19-year-olds achieving NVQ Level 3 or its equivalent by the year 2000. Yet clear strategies for achieving this target have not been identified. There is some evidence from Europe that participation rates are crucially dependent on the relationship between education and the labour market. In Germany the participation at 16/17 is 94 per cent, at 17/18 80 per cent, the simple fact being that young people in Germany up to age 18 cannot find employment with attractive remuneration. Increased participation will only be a reality if the labour market in this country is not a source

Table 11.1 Participation rates in full-time education 16–19 in selected countries

	Age 16/17		Age 17/18		Age 18/19	
	M	F	M	F	M	F
Australia	70.2	75.2	57.7	60.5	29.0	29.7
Belgium	91.2	93.3	88.1	89.3	67.4	69.0
Canada	92.4	92.5	75.6	75.3	56.4	56.3
Denmark	90.4	92.4	76.9	78.8	68.6	67.5
France	80.3	85.1	69.3	76.7	57.9	63.6
Germany	94.8	93.9	81.7	79.8	67.7	64.9
Italy*	54.0**		47.0**		41.0**	
Japan	89.8**		87.6**		50.0**	
Netherlands	93.4	92.8	79.2	77.7	59.7	57.6
Spain	64.7	66.3	55.9	58.3	30.4	27.4
Sweden	80.8**		83.1**		44.1**	
UK+	51.3	54.8	33.7	36.6	18.8	18.6
USA	94.6	94.4	88.6	88.9	57.3	53.5

*   1986
**   male and female
+   England, Wales and Scotland aggregated. There are
    higher participation rates in Scotland than in England and
    Wales.

of incentives for young people to leave education. Intervention by Government may well be required, yet only one political party has this on its agenda.

The experience in the Scottish system suggests that increased participation could be aided if opportunities were made available to gain intermediate nationally recognized qualifications. In Scotland in 1988, 50 per cent of young people were already achieving the equivalent of NVQ Level 3 qualifications compared to 20 per cent in England and Wales. The increased retention is almost certainly due to a flexible system post-16 with accreditation at age 17. A further piece of evidence to support the value of intermediate qualifications must surely be the retention rate from the BTEC First Diploma, where almost 60 per cent of the students are retained in education for a further two years. The pressure for an accredited exit route at age 17 in England and Wales has, however, fallen on deaf ears in the political arena.

Another major issue which needs to be addressed to increase participation rates and student achievement is the suitability and range of courses on offer. Young people will only remain in an education system if it is attractive, if it is accessible, if it caters for a wide range of abilities, if it is flexible and if success is the reality for the majority. Ten years after the MacFarlane report of 1980 (DES, 1980), there had been a startling increase in the range of vocational courses, with the introduction of the

Certificate of Prevocational Education as well as a system of National Vocational Qualifications based mainly in FE. In sharp contrast the only addition to the Advanced Level curriculum has been the introduction of the AS examination. The result is that education post-16 has become narrow and divisive and increasingly inappropriate to the majority of young people. This is in spite of several major attempts through Higginson and the SEAC report of 1990 to rationalize and restructure the Advanced Level curriculum. Since the failure of the latest attempt to reorganize and broaden the Advanced Level curriculum, the national debate on the need for a coherent system of qualifications has not stopped, but has in fact gained momentum.

In 1989 the CBI in an attempt to give parity of esteem to vocational courses put forward proposals to establish equivalence between vocational and academic qualifications (see Table 11.2).

Table 11.2 Proposed equivalences between vocational and academic qualifications

NVQ Level	Example of vocational qualification	'Academic' qualification	CBI targets for 16-19 age group
5	Professional institute exam	University degree	
4	Technician or management diploma (HND)	Diploma in HE	
3	BTEC National Diploma **Advanced**	2 A levels	By 2000, 50 per cent achieve this level
2	BTEC First **General**	5 GCSEs at C or above	By 1995, all young people attain this level
1	Basic Test of Practical Competence **Foundation**	A range of GCSEs	

There have been further proposals which have recommended a restructuring of the system to improve coherence. The 1991 Royal Society of Arts report, *Learning Pays,* emphasized the need to restructure the present system and to introduce an adequate curriculum for pupils of all ability with improved status for vocational courses. A central theme was the need for better guidance and counselling to assist students in making informed decisions through complex and baffling routes.

In their report *The Way Forward* (Kidd, 1991) SHA proposed a mainly modular integrated approach developed from existing academic and vocational provision which delayed final choice until age 17, mixed theoretical and applied approaches and made breadth inescapable. The document also put forward proposals for establishing equivalence between courses and on how to make the system more flexible and hence adaptable to a wider ability range.

A further report, *Beyond GCSE*, by The Royal Society (1991) recommended three compulsory domains of study which would all include skills, competences, knowledge and understanding. The three were social, economic and industrial, scientific, mathematical and technological, and creative, linguistic and aesthetic. Courses would have a modular structure and provide short-term targets and facilities for credit transfer. The system would be based on a single curriculum framework and students would have their entitlement defined in terms of skills, competences, relevant knowledge and understanding and include common features such as career guidance and work experience.

The Institute for Public Policy Research document (Finegold *et al.*, 1990) also advocates three compulsory domains similar to the Royal Society with each containing three types of modules: core, specialist modules and work/community based. The unified qualification, the British Baccalaureat would subsume existing academic, vocational and pre-vocational qualifications. There would be a foundation stage 14–17 and an advanced stage at 18 with all provision through a modular framework.

All these proposals agree on the need to build on Key Stage 4 of the National Curriculum, to absorb the pre-vocational and vocational awards into a cumulative system at 17 and 18, and the need for flexibility to accommodate students with different speeds of learning. Furthermore, the need to provide students with the opportunity to progress in areas of study at a variety of levels was recognized, as was the need for multiple entry and exit routes.

The Conservative Government singularly failed to accept any of these proposals for the simple reason that the Advanced Level system would have to be altered. In spite of less entrenched positions on the part of powerful groups such as the Head Masters Conference and the Committee of Vice-Chancellors and Principals there remained a deep suspicion that significant change to Advanced Levels would mean a decline in depth, rigour and hence standards. This overarching concern to maintain the A Level tradition has resulted in lost opportunities to achieve the laudable goals published in the 1991 White Paper:

- to ensure that high quality further education and training becomes the norm for all 16- and 17-year-olds who can benefit from it.;
- to increase the all-round levels of attainment of young people;

●to increase the proportion of young people acquiring higher-level skills.

The Government's insistence that A Levels must be retained in their existing format has led to proposals which will only serve to accentuate the academic/vocational divide. The following analysis is illustrative of the different approaches being adopted, shown in Table 11.3

Table 11.3 The vocational/academic divide

Academic	Vocational
A single subject approach	Course team approach
Assessment of core skills incidental except for innovative syllabuses such as Geography 16–19 and Wessex A/AS	Assessment of core skills an essential and integral part of all courses (BTEC Core Skills)
Project/essays are subject-based	Some attempt to integrate knowledge across the course using integrated assignments
Some modularization, e.g. 45 hr and 60 hr modules.	Modules or units for BTEC 60 hrs
Some work experience, work shadowing and projects being promoted under TVEI	Work related assignments
Move towards criterion-referenced assessment	Move towards the assessment of job-related competence as the result of the Review of Vocational Qualifications

Initially the gap widened as the work of NCVQ emphasized the assessment of job-specific competence. More recently they have increasingly recognized the importance of assessing underpinning knowledge and understanding.

However, realizing the potential of vocational qualifications to increase participation rates and the emerging national consensus for a provision encompassing both academic and vocational elements, the Government, in 1991 White Papers, proposed a new path via General National Vocational Qualifications. These proposals only served to highlight the Conservative Government's lack of true commitment to establishing parity between different pathways because the criteria included elements which appear to have been rejected by the Government for inclusion in Advanced Level examinations. Until a government accepts that core skills, interim assessment, relevance to the world of work, modularity and the requirement to apply knowledge and skills are a necessary requirement for all courses, no parity of esteem will exist. In the interests of the future economic position of this country and the need to invest in a multi-skilled, well-educated workforce, the sacred cow must be sacrificed.

There have been many attempts to subvert this sacred cow mainly through TVEI funding where modular courses, coursework and internal assessment were introduced. These ingredients are seen by many as necessary reforms in the Advanced Level system. The Government however, through restrictions on the extent of the contribution of coursework to terminal assessment, have succeeded in frustrating further development in these areas.

By not responding to the pressure for reform, the Government has failed to address the weaknesses of and the wastage in the present system. Forty per cent of 16-year-olds gain four or more GCSE passes at grades A–C, yet less than 20 per cent gain 2 A Levels or accreditation in vocational courses at NVQ Level 3. Twenty-five per cent fail A Level examinations with no record of any achievement beyond 16 and a further 5 per cent drop out of A Level study after one year. The need for interim accreditation, the need for transferability and flexibility in provision is clear; the failure of the present system to deliver is also clear.

Confusion is further highlighted in the debate on breadth in the curriculum. All vocational qualifications include the assessment of core skills as an integral part of courses and the new general vocational qualifications will also include the assessment of core skills at a variety of levels. The National Curriculum Council's document on core skills in 16–19 courses (NCC, 1990a) was accepted by the then Secretary of State, John MacGregor, but has been treated with suspicion by his successors. The same lack of continuity appears to be the reason why the invitation from John MacGregor to SEAC to review the principles associated with the A/AS examination have found little support. The rejection of this report has effectively prevented the one initiative for encouraging greater breadth developed by the Government from taking a more significant role. Furthermore, the rejection of the report ensured that many young people will still embark on a route not suitable to their needs, with no mechanism for transfer to alternative paths. The Government lost an ideal opportunity to make breadth in Advanced Level study a reality when it failed to highlight the need for assessment criteria for making the possession of a wide range of core skills above National Curriculum Level 8 a prerequisite for obtaining its proposed National Diploma. The issue of breadth in the academic curriculum is once more left to institutions who are required to innovate with programmes of general studies, additional studies or complementary studies. The result is that schools and colleges are faced with programmes which are difficult to sell to students, not because of lack of quality but because of lack of national currency.

After 10 years of debate, two substantial reports on the Advanced Level system and innovation through TVEI funding, the brakes have been firmly put on the reform of Advanced Level. Also after 10 years of debate, there are now more vocational courses culminating in two different national awards and little parity of esteem. The 'jungle' referred to by Eric Bolton (HMI, 1990b) has become a reality.

Because of the lost opportunities, the only way forward must now be through significant change; the following criteria are vital if it is to take place.

Criteria for Change

1. One body must be responsible for education and training in Britain. The present split between the Department of Employment and the Department of Education and Science only serves to exacerbate the academic and vocational path, a fact identified by Eric Bolton in his last report as HM Senior Chief Inspector of Schools (HMI, 1990b):

   Post 16 education is a confused and confusing scene in terms of institutions and curricula. It receives funding from a variety of sources and is subject to policy from both the Department of Education and Science and the Department of Employment. Schools, colleges HE institutions and employers are uncertain about the overall rationale for post 16 provision.

2. Academic and vocational education and training must cease to exist as separate identities. There should be an overarching qualification, the National Diploma, which accredits attainment at an agreed level through a variety of paths.

3. The principles covering academic and vocational course design should be the same; only the weightings given to each constituent should vary (Kidd, 1991). This process would give a mechanism for assessing equivalence, aid credit transfer and ensure parity of esteem between courses. Courses could be mainly theory-based or practically-based and the complete student programme would be negotiated on an indi-

vidual basis, combining the most suitable and relevant courses from the range offered. This process already works to the advantage of students in Scotland who combine Highers with SCOTVEC modules.

4. The features of good practice developed within GCSE examinations which include a range of assessment strategies and coursework requirements and which have served to motivate more students to continue in education should inform the planning of developments post-16. However, many students still see GCSE as an end-of-education examination. Nationally, this perception must be removed by retaining the best practice in GCSE assessment in the assessment of Key Stage 4 and continuing this assessment beyond Level 10.

5. Planning for progression throughout the system and, in particular, building on the National Curriculum Key Stages must be a priority. Attainment levels should be increased (SHA, 1989) but all qualifications after the compulsory school age should cease to be age-related. Students should be able to combine courses from a variety of levels, the number of courses being subject to agreement with the student after appropriate guidance.

6. All achievement should be recorded on a National Record of Achievement which is the negotiating tool for further education, training or employment.

7. The system of qualifications should give students choice and flexibility but should make breadth inescapable. The core skills identified by NCC, SEAC and NCVQ should be incorporated into all programmes of study and should be assessed.

8. All post-compulsory programmes of study should provide the same progression routes, into continuing education or training or employment. Students must be able to see a well-signposted path through the system. This depends on quality careers guidance and counselling.

9. Employers must be included in discussions on education and training. There must be a supportive partnership between educationalists and employers and a mutual understanding of the economic needs of the nation. Government will have to assist in this process by either giving young people financial incentives to remain in education or training or offering disincentives to employers who take young people out of education at age 16.

The achievement of these criteria will critically depend on a significant rationalization and reorganization of existing structures:

1. There must be one government department responsible for funding education and training.

2. The National Curriculum Council, the Secondary Examinations and

Assessment Council and the National Council for Vocational Qualifications should be reorganized into one, a National Awarding Body for all qualifications with, perhaps, a national body giving advice on curriculum matters.

3. The number of examination boards and vocational bodies should be reduced. The present large number contributes to expensive examination fees and a jungle of awards and syllabuses. With fewer boards, reasonable choice can be still maintained.

4. The role of the TECS must be strengthened and steps taken to bring many more employers into the education/training forum.

A political cross-roads has been reached in 16–19 education. Change has been thwarted by a Government which has not established a clear and coherent route for development. The Government's aims as expressed in the 1991 White Paper were laudable, but cannot be achieved whilst there is an insistence on retaining the status quo with regard to the Advanced Level examination. The Government's determination to achieve this latter goal will result in the sacrifice of the AS examination, perpetuate confusion in the vocational field and ensure the continuance of a dual system. One simple manoeuvre, the requirement that all students start on a five- or six-subject base at 16, not only would have increased uptake of the AS examination but also would have made increased breadth for students undertaking a theory-based programme a reality. Such a move first postulated by Higginson would give flexibility for students either to continue in their first year post-16 with a five-subject broad base or allow more in-depth study through taking a smaller number of Advanced Levels (Kidd, 1991). The result could be a system similar in philosophy to the International Baccalaureat. Furthermore, as in Scotland, there would be an opportunity to mix theoretical and vocational courses and the system could cater, again as the Scottish system does, for students of a wide range of abilities by allowing them to take fewer courses. Such a change would move the system towards the unified approach now accepted by many as the only way to cure the ills of the present system.

As the end of the century approaches, future developments in 16–19 education will unfortunately depend on the politics of the party in power. Sadly, education in this country has been removed from educationalists into the hands of Secretaries of State made more powerful by much of the legislation enacted in the 1980s. Already it has been shown by events detailed in this book that, even within the same political party, Secretaries of State can change drastically what their predecessors have accepted and introduced. This has been the reality with the core skills debate initiated by Kenneth Baker, accepted by John MacGregor and practically dismissed by Kenneth Clarke. Sadly this means that the coherent planning which the system needs may never be realized.

The politicizing of education is clearly not to the advantage of our young people but this lesson appears not to have been learnt. If in power it is likely that one party will retain the present system with its jungle of qualifications and divisive nature, another will certainly overhaul the system and legislate for education or training to be compulsory after 16, while the third may wish to reform the system but may not in the end have the boldness to carry out their stated aims. Two parties will support the establishment of tertiary education, with LEAs responsible for strategic planning, the third will isolate LEAs and will centrally fund a new sector which will be responsible for 50 per cent of all full-time students 16–19. How can teachers, governors and LEAs plan for quality provision when there is so much uncertainty about the future?

The 1980s and early 1990s have been characterized by the number of opportunities for significant change in 16–19 education, and the fact that many of these have proved to be lost opportunities. It is clear that amongst the majority of educationalists and teachers there is a consensus on the need for a unified flexible system of provision post–16 and that this consensus is now increasingly supported by those in industry. How long must we wait for its implementation?

Abbreviations and Acronyms

AS   **Advanced Supplementary** – introduced by the DES in 1984 these courses are judged at the same standard as an Advanced Level but as taking up half the teaching time. They have remained a key part of the DES's strategy for broadening the 'academic' curriculum post-16.

BTEC   **Business and Technician Education Council** – established in 1983 (by the merger of TEC and BEC, formed 1973-4), BTEC offers a range of work-related qualifications at different levels. The subjects covered include business and finance, computing, design, hotel and catering, management and leisure studies. It provides a progressive framework of 'technician-level' courses: BTEC First Certificates/Diplomas; BTEC National Certificates/Diplomas (broadly equivalent to A Levels); BTEC Higher National Certificates/Diplomas (just below degree level).

CBI   **Confederation of British Industry** – is the largest central employers' organization in Britain, representing directly or indirectly some 250,000 businesses which together employ about half the working population.

CEE   **Certificate in Extended Education** – introduced in 1973, this was a one year course available in a number of individual subjects which led to a CEE examination administered by the Certificate of Secondary Education examining boards. It was to be replaced by the new CPVE but several examining boards resisted pressure to drop it in favour of CPVE. This is no longer available.

CPVE   **Certificate of Pre-Vocational Education** – was initiated in
1984 under joint BTEC and CGLI management (*see*
JBPVE). The CPVE framework (revised in September
1989) comprises three components – **The Core** (five areas –
Communication and Social Skills; Applied Numeracy;
Problem Solving; Science, Technology and Information
Technology; Social, Industrial and Economic Awareness);
Vocational Studies (five categories – Business and
Administrative Services; Technical Services; Production;
Distribution; Services to People); **Additional Studies** (not
mandatory, but might include GCSEs and community activities, recreation, leisure). Courses normally last one year
and must include at least 15 days of real or simulated work
experience and must also include formal provision for
planned and regular guidance and counselling. The emphasis is on integration of components and areas of study,
although the design and balance of courses rest largely with
individual schools or colleges. CPVE programmes can be
followed in conjunction with courses leading to various
other qualifications, including A Levels (over two years).
This is in the process of being replaced by the Diploma in
Vocational Education.

CGLI   **City and Guilds of London Institute** – was founded in
1878 by the City of London and its Livery Companies. It is
an independent, self-governing and self-financing body constituted for the advancement of technical education. It is the
largest body awarding vocational qualifications in England.
It awards certificates for vocational and pre-vocational studies, traditionally at 'craft' and 'operative' levels in colleges
of further education (*see* BTEC, JBPVE, CPVE, DoVE),
but with an increasing involvement in secondary schools.

DE   **Department of Employment** – responsible for the government policy of promoting a competitive and efficient labour
market conducive to the growth of employment and the
reduction of unemployment. Its main tasks are to help people acquire and improve their skills and competence for
work, to help unemployed people, to promote the creation
of and growth of small firms and self-employment, to
encourage industries to train their workforce and to develop
tourism. In 1988 it was renamed the Employment
Department (ED).

DES   **Department of Education and Science** – its main responsibilities are the general promotion of education, the government's relations with British universities and fostering civil science in Britain and internationally.

DoVE   **Diploma of Vocational Education** – it was announced by the CGLI in June 1991 that CPVE and Foundation Programmes pre-16 would be replaced by a Diploma of Vocational Education. It will cover the 14–19 age range and will have three levels, Foundation, Intermediate and National. It is intended to link the accreditation with GNVQs.

DTI   **Department of Trade and Industry** – its main responsibilities are industrial and commercial policy, including: industrial innovation policy; patents; international trade policy; commercial relations and export promotion; competition policy; company law; insolvency; consumer protection and safety, and the sponsorship of manufacturing and service industries.

ED   **Employment Department** – *see* Department of Employment (DE).

ET   **Employment Training** – set out in the White Paper *Training for Employment* (DE, 1988), the scheme provides up to 12 months training for those who have been unemployed for more than six months (with priority given to 18- to 24-year-olds and to those between 18 and 50 who have been unemployed for more than two years).

FE   **Further Education** – up until recently this referred, strictly speaking, to all post-school education excluding universities, but was generally used to refer to non-advanced further education (NAFE) as distinct from advanced further education. These administrative distinctions will be radically altered as a result of the White Papers *Education and Training for the 21st Century* (DES/DE, 1991a; 1991b) and *Higher Education: A New Framework* (DES/DE, 1991c).

FEU   **Further Education Unit** – set up in 1975 as part of the DES, the FEU became an independent body at the start of 1983, though still funded by the DES. It was established to promote, encourage and develop Further Education. The FEU is involved in four main areas of activity: the evaluation of existing provision; the recommendation of improvements; the undertaking of research and the evaluation of initiatives; the publication of information on FE developments.

G(N)VQ **General (National) Vocational Qualification** – proposed in the White Paper *Education and Training for the 21st Century* (DES/DE, 1991a; 1991b), G(N)VQs, unlike **NVQ**s, will not involve acquiring specific occupational skills (assessed in the work-place) and are part of recent reforms aimed at bridging the academic/vocational divide. Courses leading to the award of G(N)VQs can be run by secondary schools and are due to commence in September 1992 (*see* NCVQ, NVQ)

HE **Higher Education** – the system responsible for courses followed in advanced further education (AFE) or the university sector, where the level of instruction is above that of GCE A Level or equivalent. The funding and administration of this sector will be radically affected when the proposals contained in the White Paper *Higher Education: A New Framework* (DES/DE, 1991c) come into effect in 1993.

JBPVE **Joint Board for Pre-Vocational Education** – established on a DES initiative by BTEC and CGLI to oversee CPVE.

LIB **Lead Industry Body** – designated by the Training Agency, LIBs set standards for education/training in occupational areas. These standards form the bases for NVQs. For example, the Hotel and Catering Training Board (HCTB) is the LIB responsible for setting standards of occupational competence which will form the basis for vocational qualifications in the hotel and catering sector (*see* NVQ, TA).

MSC **Manpower Services Commission** – established under the Employment and Training Act 1973 to undertake the Department of Employment's responsibilities for training and employment exchanges. It had three major operating divisions: Employment Services Division (ESD), Training Services Division (TSD), Special Programmes Division (SPD) (*see* TA).

NAFE **Non-Advanced Further Education** – *see* FE, WRNAFE.

NCC **National Curriculum Council** – set up by the 1988 Education Reform Act, the Council advises the Secretary of State on the development of the National Curriculum and supports teachers and schools in the implementation of the curriculum (ages 5–19) in partnership with other agencies.

NCVQ **National Council for Vocational Qualifications** – set up on 1 Oct 1986 to establish a coherent national framework, with clear paths of progression, for vocational qualifications. The framework consists of five levels which extend

142

from basic skills to professional qualifications.. The target date for coverage of all occupational sectors within the NCVQ framework qualifications is 1992.

NROVA   **National Record of Vocational Achievement** – the record of experience and qualifications gained within the NCVQ framework, intended to provide coherence and facilitate progression.

NTI   **New Training Initiative** – a proposal for improvements to training submitted for consideration by the MSC in 1981. It had three objectives: to provide a properly organized system of retraining opportunities for adults, to replace apprenticeship with skill-based training and to organize appropriate combinations of work experience and training for all school leavers.

NVQ   **National Vocational Qualification** – a qualification which has been accredited as fulfilling the criteria of the NCVQ framework. An NVQ is composed of a number of units of competence, each capable of being separately recorded. Each unit is broken down into smaller parts called 'elements of competence', accompanied by performance criteria indicating the standard required for competent performance of specified occupational skills.

OTF   **Occupational Training Families** – a broad-based classification of occupations in terms of training required (replaced by TOC).

RSA   **Royal Society of Arts** – examining body concerned mainly with commercial education and a major provider of curricula and examinations in clerical and secretarial skills.

RVQ   **Review of Vocational Qualifications** – a review group set up as a result of recommendations in the 1985 White Paper *Education and Training for Young People* (DES/DE). The group was given the task of recommending a structure of vocational qualifications which would be relevant to the needs of people with a wide range of abilities. Its final report in 1986 called for a National Council of Vocational Qualifications (NCVQ) to rationalize and extend vocational qualifications and to ensure that the qualifications were relevant to employment needs.

SEAC **Schools Examination and Assessment Council** –was set up by the 1988 Education Reform Act to advise the Secretary of State on the most appropriate means of assessing children's attainment in the National Curriculum. It has been charged with producing test materials – Standard Assessment Tasks (SATs) to be used as children reach certain Key Stages in their education.

SSS **Supported Self Study** – resource/assignment-based learning pursued in conjuction with planned tutorial support.

TA **Training Agency** – new name given to the MSC in 1988 (after a brief period as the Training Commission). It was disbanded in Autumn 1990 and many of its areas of responsibility devolved to the Training and Enterprise Councils (TECs). Remaining TA activities were incorporated within the Employment Department, merging with existing functions under a new name – the Training, Enterprise and Education Directorate (*see* MSC, TEED).

TEC **Training and Enterprise Council** – established in April 1990, TECs are employer-led boards with responsibility for the planning of vocational education and training (including YT and ET) on a local basis . TECs will also influence schools and sixth form colleges through TVEI.

TEED **Training, Enterprise and Education Directorate** – section of the Employment Department which took over responsibilities for educational funding from the Training Agency (*see* TA, MSC).

TOC **Training Occupations Classification** – defines occupations according to the type of training required (e.g., Administrative/Clerical; Hotel, Catering and Food Preparation). Each TOC determines the range of skills needed within the relevant occupation(s) and the relative importance of these skills. (Replaced OTF.)

TUC **Trades Union Congress** – founded in 1868, is a voluntary association of trade unions, the representatives of which meet annually to consider matters of common concern to their members.

TVEI **Technical and Vocational Education Initiative** – an MSC initiative to fund curriculum development in schools and colleges emphasizing preparation for the world of work for the 14–18 age range.

UVP   **Unified Vocational Preparation** – sponsored by Training Services Division of MSC, catered for young people at work not normally in receipt of education or training (pilot scheme: 1977). Day/block release – vocational skills, social and life skills. Later incorporated into YTS.

WRNAFE   **Work-related Non-advanced Further Education** (*see* NAFE, FE) – in 1985–6 the government transferred a quarter of the overall funding for work-related FE courses in FE colleges from local authorities' budgets to the MSC. Initially, each authority received back from the MSC, for WRNAFE, a sum roughly equal to the amount deducted from its grant. To obtain these funds, each local authority had to submit three-year plans for their provision of WRNAFE, for approval by the Department of Employment in the light of its judgement about training needs and appropriate methods of meeting them.

YOP   **Youth Opportunities Programme** – introduced by the SPD of the MSC in April 1978 as a programme of training and work experience for unemployed young people (superseded by YTS).

YT   **Youth Training** – replaced YTS in 1990. Funded by ED through the Training and Entreprise Councils on a regional basis (*see* TEC).

YTS   **Youth Training Scheme** – initiated in September 1983, the scheme is aimed at 16-year-old school-leavers who are unemployed during their first year after leaving school. A new system of delivery, originally a one-year course, that was extended to two years, YTS(2), from April 1986. Now replaced by Youth Training (*see* YT).

References

Ainley, P. (1990) *Vocational Education and Training*, London: Cassell.

Ainley, P. and Corney, M. (1990) *Training for the Future: The Rise and Fall of the Manpower Services Commission*, London: Cassell.

ALEP (Advanced Level Enhancement Project) (1989) *Aspects of Entitlement*, Occasional Paper No. 1, Leicestershire Local Education Authority.

Anderson, E. (1991) 'Change is not as good as a test', *Times Educational Supplement*, 21 June, p.11.

Ashton, D. and Lowe, G. (1991) *Making Their Way: Education, Training and the Labour Market in Canada and Britain*, Milton Keynes: Open University Press.

Ashton, D.N. and Maguire, M.J. (1986) *Young Adults in the Labour Market*, Department of Employment Research Paper No. 55.

Ashton, D., Maguire, M.J., Maguire, S. and Sutton, A. (1989) *Developing Education and Training Links for the 14–19 Age Group*, Sheffield: Training Agency.

Ashton, D.N., Maguire, M.J. and Spilsbury, M. (1990) *Restructuring the Labour Market: The Implications for Youth*, Basingstoke: Macmillan.

Avis, J. (1990) 'Some reflections on the core curriculum', *Liberal Education*, 67 p.20

Baines, P., Broadfoot, P. and Nuttall, D. (1989) *Final Report of the Profiling in TVEI Research Project*, Sheffield: Employment Department.

Baker, K. (1989) *Further Education: A New Strategy*, London: DES.

Ball, C., Sir (1991a) 'Introduction and Conclusions and Summary', in *Lifelong Learning: Britain's Future*, a conference report Employment Department/University of Oxford.

Ball, C., Sir (1991b) *Learning Pays: The Role of Post-Compulsory Education and Training*, interim report by Sir Christopher Ball, London: Royal Society of Arts.

Ball, C., Sir (1991c) 'Papering over the cracks,' *Education Guardian*, 28 May, p.21.

Ball, C., Sir (1991d) 'Ways out of a fools' paradise,' *Times Educational Supplement*, 19 May, p.16.

Barnes, D., Johnson, G., Jordan, S., Layton, D., Medway, P. and Yeomans, D.

(1987) *The TVEI Curriculum: an interim report based on case studies in twelve schools*, Leeds: University of Leeds School of Education.

Barnett, C. (1972) *The Collapse of British Power*, London: Eyre Methuen.

Barnett, C. (1986) *The Audit of War: The illusion and reality of Britain as a great nation*, Basingstoke: Macmillan.

Bees, M. and Swords M. (eds) (1990) *National Vocational Qualifications and Further Education*, London: Kogan Page and NCVQ.

Black, H. and Wolf, A. (eds) (1990) *Knowledge and Competence: Current Issues in Training and Education*, London: Employment Department.

Board of Education (1939) *Report of the Consultative Committee on Secondary Education with Special Reference to Grammar Schools and Technical High Schools*, London: HMSO.

Boffy, R. (1990a) 'Diversity is essential to a common core', *Times Educational Supplement*, 19 January.

Boffy, R. (1990b) 'Occupational competence and work-based learning: the future for further education?', in Bees, M. and Swords M. (eds) *National Vocational Qualifications and Further Education*, London: Kogan Page and NCVQ.

Broadfoot, P. (ed.) (1984) *Selection, Certification and Control*, London: Falmer Press.

Broadfoot, P. (1986a) 'Profiling and the affective curriculum', *Journal of Curriculum Studies*, **19**, 1, 25–34.

Broadfoot, P. (ed.) (1986b) *Profiles and Records of Achievement: A Review of Issues and Practice*, Eastbourne: Holt, Rinehart and Winston.

Broadfoot, P. (1987) *Introducing Profiling*, Basingstoke: Macmillan.

Broadfoot, P., James, M., McMeeking, S., Nuttall, D. and Stierer, B. (1988) *Records of Achievement: Report of the National Evaluation of Pilot Schemes*, London: HMSO.

Broadfoot, P., Grant, M., James, M., Nuttall, D. and Stierer, B. (1991) *Records of Achievement: Report of the National Evaluation of Extension Work in Pilot Schemes*, London: HMSO.

BTEC (1984) *Policies and Priorities into the 1990s*, London: BTEC.

BTEC/CGLI (1988) *CPVE – Evaluation, General Findings and Recommendations*, London: BTEC/CGLI.

Burrage, H. (1991) 'The National Curriculum at 16+', *Social Science Teacher*, **20**, 2, 49–50

Bynner, J. (1991) 'Transitions to work: results from a longitudinal study of young people in four British labour markets', pp. 171–95, in Ashton, D. and Lowe, G. *Making Their Way: Education, Training and the Labour Market in Canada and Britain*, Milton Keynes: Open University Press.

Cantor, L.M. and Roberts, I.F. (1986) *Further Education Today: A Critical Review* (3rd edn.), London: Routledge and Kegan Paul.

Cassels, J. (1990) *Britain's Real Skill Shortage and What to Do about it*, Discussion Papers of the Policy Studies Institute, No. 30.

CBI (1989) *Towards a Skills Revolution:* Report of the Vocational Education and Training Task Force, London: CBI.

CBI (1991) *World Class Targets*, London: CBI.

CBI and NCVQ (1990) *National Targets and the Implications for NVQ Levels*, London: CBI and NCVQ.

Chitty, C. (ed.) (1991) *Post-16 Education: Studies in Access and Achievement*, London: Kogan Page.

City and Guilds (1991) *Diploma of Vocational Education Information*, London: CGLI.

Clarke, K. (1991a) Speech to the Annual Conference of SHA.

Clarke, K. (1991b) Statement on the Reorganization of FE.

Clarke,K. (1991c) 'Staying on in education and training', address given to the Annual General meeting of The Association of Colleges for Further and Higher Education, London, 20/21 February.

Coates, P (1990) *The Core Skills Initiative*, report to the 16–19 Curriculum Study Group, London: FEU.

Coates, P (1991) 'The 16-19 core skills initiative', *The Curriculum Journal*, **2**, 1, 43–53.

Coffield, F. (1990) 'From the decade of the enterprise culture to the decade of the TECs', *British Journal of Education and Work*, **4**, 1, 59–79.

Committee on Higher Education (1963) *Higher Education. Report of the Committee on Higher Education under the Chairmanship of Lord Robbins, 1961-3*, London: HMSO.

Coopers and Lybrand (1985) *A Challenge to Complacency: Changing Attitudes to Training*, Sheffield: Manpower Services Commission.

Dale, R. (1983) 'Thatcherism and education', in Ahier, J. and Flude, M.(eds.) *Contemporary Education Policy*, Beckenham: Croom Helm.

Dancy J. (ed.) (1984) *Perspectives 14: TVEI*, University of Exeter.

DE (1981) *New Training Initiative: A Programme for Action*, London: HMSO.

DE (1984) *Training for Jobs*, London: HMSO.

DE (1988) *Employment for the 1990s*, London: HMSO.

DE (1989) *Training in Britain*, London: HMSO.

DE (1990) *Flexible Learning in Schools*, Sheffield: Employment Department.

DE (1991) *Flexible Learning: A Framework for Education and Training in the Skills Decade*, Sheffield: Employment Department.

DE/DES (1986) *Working Together – Education and Training*, London: HMSO.

DES (1969) *Report of the Committee on Technician Courses and Exams* (Haslegrave Report), London: DES.

DES (1979) *Proposals for a Certificate of Extended Education*, Chair Professor K.W.Keohane, London: HMSO.

DES (1980) *Education for 16–19 Year Olds: A Review Undertaken for the Government and the Local Authority Associations*, London: HMSO.

DES (1982) *17+ A New Qualification*, London: HMSO.

DES (1983) *Vocational Further Education Through the 1980s*, Report of an Invitation Conference arranged by HMI, London: HMSO.

DES (1984a) *AS Levels: Proposals by the Secretaries of State for Education and*

148

Science and Wales for a Broader Curriculum for A Level Students, London: HMSO.

DES (1984b) *Records of Achievement; A Statement of Policy*, London: HMSO.

DES (1985) *Better Schools*, cm.9469, London: HMSO.

DES (1987) *Broadening A Level Studies – Advanced Supplementary (AS) Levels: A Guide for Schools and Colleges*, London: HMSO.

DES (1988) *Advancing A Levels*, Report of a Committee appointed by the Secretary of State for Education and Science and the Secretary of State for Wales (The Higginson Report), London: HMSO.

DES (1989a) *GCE Advanced Supplementary Examinations: The First Two Years*, a report by HM Inspectorate, London: HMSO.

DES (1989b) *Records of Achievement ; Report of the National Steering Committee on Records of Achievement*, London: DES

DES (1989c) *Further Education: A New Strategy*, speech by Kenneth Baker to the Conference of ACFHE, London: HMSO.

DES (1990) *Standards in Education 1988–89*, The Annual Report of HM Senior Chief Inspector of Schools, London: HMSO.

DES (1991a) *Programmes of Students on GCE A and AS Level Courses*, a report by HM Inspectorate, London: HMSO.

DES (1991b) *Ordinary and Advanced Diplomas. A Consultation Document*, London: DES.

DES/DE (1985) *Education and Training for Young People*, cm. 9482, London: HMSO.

DES/DE (1991a) *Education and Training for the 21st Century, Volume One*, cm.1536, London: HMSO.

DES/DE (1991b) *Education and Training for the 21st Century, Volume Two, The Challenge to Colleges*, cm.1536, London: HMSO.

DES/DE (1991c) *Higher Education: A New Framework*, cm. 1541, London: HMSO.

DES News (1990a) *A Levels – speech by John MacGregor*, Press Release 356/90, London: DES.

DES News (1990b) *Science Further Education needs both A Levels and vocational qualifications*, Press Release 387/90, London: DES.

DES News (1990c) *Schools to offer an alternative route to higher education*, Press Release 396/90, London: DES.

DES News (1991) *NCVQ asked to develop broader based qualifications*, Press Release 162/91, London: DES.

D'Hooghe, D.A. (1984) The Role of the Manpower Services Commission in the Development of Education Policy for 16–19 Year Olds, M.Sc. thesis, University of Oxford, unpublished.

Duffy, M. (1989) 'Broadly speaking', *Times Educational Supplement*, 6 January, p.13.

ED (1990) *Flexible Learning in Schools*, Sheffield: Employment Department.

ED (1991a) *Developing Good Practice: Assessment, Guidance and Action Planning*, Sheffield: Employment Department.

149

ED (1991b) *The Flexible Approach to Learning. A Guide*, Sheffield: Employment Department.

ED (1991c) *Youth Development Project Directory*, Sheffield: Employment Department.

ED/NRA (1991) *Recording Achievement and Planning Individual Development. Guidance in Summarising the Record and Completing the National Record of Achievement*, Sheffield: Employment Department.

ED/TVEI (1991) *Guidance for those Managing TVEI: Recording Achievement and Planning Individual Development*, Sheffield: Employment Department.

Education (1990) 'Mrs Rumbold tiptoes through the tulips of the core curriculum', editorial, **175**, 14, 333–4.

Edwards, A. (1983) 'The reconstruction of post-compulsory education and training in England and Wales', *European Journal of Education*, **18**, 1, 7–20.

FEU (1979) *A Basis For Choice*, London: FEU.

FEU (1981) *ABC in Action*, a report from an FEU/CGLI working party on the piloting of 'A Basis for Choice', 1979–81, Stanmore: FECRDU.

FEU (1983) *Supporting YTS*, London: FEU.

FEU (1985) *Signposts 85: A Review of 16–19 Education*, London: FEU.

FEU (1987) *Relevance, Flexibility and Competence*, London: FEU.

FEU (1988) *Planning the FE Curriculum: Implications of the 1988 Education Reform Act*, London: FEU.

FEU (1989a) *National Vocational Qualifications and Further Education: A Commentary on Progress*, London: FEU.

FEU (1989b) *Towards a Framework for Curriculum Entitlement*, London: FEU.

FEU (1990) *The Core Skills Initiative*, London: FEU.

Finegold, D. and Soskice, D. (1988) 'The failure of training in Britain: analysis and prescription', *Oxford Review of Economic Policy*, **4**, 3, 21–53.

Finegold, D., Keep, E., Miliband, D., Raffe, D., Spours, K. and Young, M. (1990) *A British 'Baccalaureat': Ending the Division between Education and Training*, London Institute for Public Policy Research No. 1

Fitz-Gibbon, C.T., Hazelwood, R.D., Tymms, P.B. and McCabe, J.J.C. (1988) 'Performance indicators and the TVEI pilot', *Evaluation and Research in Education*, **2**, 2, 49–60

Gleeson, D. (ed.) (1987) *TVEI and Secondary Education: A Critical Appraisal*, Milton Keynes: Open University Press.

Goss, T., and Thomann, P. E. (1991) *Destinations of BTEC Diploma Students*, BTEC: London.

Gretton, R. (1990) 'Records of Achievement and admissions to higher education', in *North West Post 16 Network Newsletter*, 9.

Guthrie, J.W. and Pierce, L.G. (1990) 'The international economy and national economic reform: a comparison of educational reforms in the United States and Great Britain', *Oxford Review of Education*, **16**, 2, 179–205.

Haffenden, I. (1990) 'The education of 16–19 year olds', pp.325–32, in Entwistle, N. (ed.) *Handbook of Educational Ideas and Practices*, London: Routledge.

150

Hargreaves, A. (1989) 'Changes, choices and challenges in secondary education', in Clough, E., Clough, P. and Nixon, J. (eds.) *The New Learning*, Basingstoke: Macmillan.

Harland, J. (1987) 'The TVEI experience: issues of control, response and the professional role of teachers', in Gleeson, D. (ed.) *TVEI and Secondary Education: A Critical Appraisal*, Milton Keynes: Open University Press.

Harland, J. (1991) 'Upper secondary education in England and Wales: an overview of curriculum pathways', in Chitty, C. (ed.) *Post-16 Education: Studies in Access and Achievement*, London: Kogan Page.

Hayes, C., Izatt, A., Morrison, J., Smith, H. and Townsend, C. (1982) *Foundation Training Issues*, report prepared at the request of the Manpower Services Commission, Institute of Manpower Studies, 39.

Hayes, C., Fonda, N., Pope, M., Stuart, R. and Townsend, K. (1983) *Training for Skill Ownership:Learning to Take it with You*, report prepared at the request of the Manpower Services Commission, Institute of Manpower Studies, 68.

Hayes, C. (1989) *'Qualifications for an uncertain future'*, address given to the Association of Colleges for Further and Higher Education, 15/16 February.

HMI (1977) *Curriculum 11–16: A Contribution to Current Debate, Working Papers by HM Inspectorate*, London: HMSO.

HMI (1984a) *Report by HMI on St. Philip's Sixth Form College (RC Aided) Birmingham*, London: HMSO.

HMI (1984b) *Education for Employers*, London: HMSO.

HMI (1986) *A Survey of the Teaching of A Level Literature in 20 Mixed Sixth Forms in Comprehensive Schools*, London: HMSO.

HMI (1987a) *NAFE in Practice*, London: HMSO.

HMI (1987b) *Experiencing A Level – Aspects of Quality*, London: HMSO.

HMI (1988a) *A Survey of Sixth Form Colleges*, London: HMSO.

HMI (1988b) *Secondary Schools: An Appraisal by HMIs*, London: HMSO.

HMI (1989a) *A Survey of History Provision for 16–19 Year Olds*, London: HMSO.

HMI (1989b) *Post-16 Education and Training, Core Skills: An HMI Paper*, London: HMSO.

HMI (1990a) *Core Skills in Further Education*, London: DES.

HMI (1990b) *Standards in Education 1988-89. The Annual Report of the HM Senior Chief Inspector of Schools*, London: DES.

HMI (1991a) *Annual Report of HM Senior Chief Inspector of Schools 1989-90*, London: DES.

HMI (1991b) *Programmes of Students on General Certificate of Education Advanced Level Courses (AS and A Level) 1989–90*, London: HMSO.

HMI (1991c) *Technical and Vocational Education Initiative (TVEI) – England and Wales 1983–1990*, London: HMSO.

HMSO (1990) *Highly Qualified People : Supply and Demand*, report of an Interdepartmental Review, London: HMSO.

Hodkinson, P. (1991) 'Liberal education and the new vocationalism: a progressive partnership', *Oxford Review of Education* 17, 2, 73–88.

Holness, M. (1990) 'Well-rounded attainment', *Education*, **175**, 17, 414–5.

Holt, M. (ed.) (1987) *Skills and Vocationalism: The Easy Answer*, Milton Keynes: Open University Press.

House, E.R. (1979) 'Technology versus craft: a ten year perspective on innovation', *Journal of Curriculum Studies* **11**, 1, 1–17.

House of Lords Select Committee on European Communities (1990) *The Vocational Training and Retraining Report*, London: HMSO.

Institute of Manpower Studies (1984) *Competence and Competition: Training and Education in the Federal Republic of Germany, the United States and Japan*, London: NEDO/MSC.

ISJC (1989) *The Sixth Form Curriculum (AS Levels)*, two discussion papers requested by the Headmasters' Conference (HMC), London: ISJC.

Jackson, R. (1989) 'Government policy on A and AS Levels', in Hughes, J. (ed.) *AS Levels: Implications for Schools, Examining Boards and Universities*, London: Falmer Press.

Jackson, R. (1991) Speech to Conference in *Lifelong Learning: Britain's Future*, a conference report, Employment Department/University of Oxford.

Jarvis, V. and Prais, S.J. (1989) 'Two nations of shopkeepers: training for retailing in France and Britain', *National Institute Economic Review*, **128**, 58–75.

Jessup, G. (1990) *Accreditation of Prior Learning in the Context of National Vocational Qualifications*, NCVQ R&D Report 7, London: NCVQ.

Jessup, G. (1991) *Outcomes, NVQs and the Emerging Model of Education and Training*, London: Falmer Press.

Jewell, D. (1990) 'Advance on two levels', *Times Educational Supplement*, 8 June, A22.

Johnson, R. (1990) *Personnel Management*, December, p.4.

Jones, A. (1990) 'The TVEI extension post 16', in Hodkinson, P. (ed.) *TVEI and the Post 16 Curriculum*, Exeter: Wheaton Education.

Jones, K. (1989) *Right Turn: The Conservative Revolution in Education*, London: Hutchinson Radius.

Kidd, L. (1991) *16–19 The Way Forward*, Secondary Heads' Association Occasional Paper 91/1, Leicester: SHA.

Knight, C. (1990) *The Making of Tory Education Policy in Post War Britain 1950–1986*, London: Falmer Press.

Labour Party (1990) *Investing in Britain's Future*, London: The Labour Party.

Labour Party (1991) *Today's Education and Training: Tomorrow's Skills*, London: The Labour Party.

Law, B. (1984) *The Uses and Abuses of Profiling: A Handbook on Reviewing and Recording Student Experience and Achievement*, London: Harper and Row.

Lawton, D. (1989) *Education, Culture and the National Curriculum*, London: Hodder and Stoughton.

Lee, D.J., Marsden, D., Rickman, P. and Duncombe, J. (1990) *Scheming for Youth: A study of YTS in the Enterprise Culture*, Milton Keynes: Open University Press.

Leicestershire LEA (1988) *The Leicestershire Curriculum Statement – Draft*

152

Working Document , Leicestershire LEA.

Levy, M. (1987) *The Core Skills Project and Work Based Learning*, Blagdon: FESC.

Lewis, H. (1989) 'Some aspects of education in France relevant to current concerns in the United Kingdom', *Comparative Education*, **25**, 3, 369–78.

Lloyd George, D. (1936) *War Memoirs*, London: Odhams Press.

Low, G. (1990) 'A certificate for all seasons', *Education*, **175**, 17, 416–7.

MacFarlane, E. (1990) 'Solution or dilution', *Times Educational Supplement*, 5 October.

MacGregor, J. (1989) *Further Advice in Response to the Report of the SEAC Consultation (July 1989) on the Promotion of AS Examinations and the Rationalisation of A Level Syllabuses*, London: SEAC.

MacGregor, J. (1990) *Letter to SEAC*, 2 November 1990, London: DES.

Maclure, S. (1991a) 'The future of further education', speech given to Annual General Meeting of Association of Colleges for Further and Higher Education, February.

Maclure, S. (1991b) *Missing Links: The Challenge to Further Education*, London: Policy Studies Institute.

Major, J. (1991) Report of speech to the Centre for Policy Studies, 3 July.

Maurice, M., Sellier, F. and Silvestre, J.J. (1986) *The Social Foundations of Industrial Power: A Comparison of France and Germany*, Cambridge, MA: MIT Press.

Mayne, P.W. (1986) Perceptions of Teaching Strategies in the A Level Classroom, unpublished M.Ed thesis, University of Leicester.

Mayne, P.W. (1988) *Teaching and Learning Styles in the A Level Classroom: Department Awareness, Discussion and Policy Making*, mimeo, Rutland Sixth Form College.

Mayne, P.W. (1990) 'Effective Learning – pedagogy in the A Level classroom', in Everton, T., Mayne, P.W. and White, S. (eds) *Effective Learning: Into a New ERA*, London: David Fulton.

Micklewright, J., Pearson, M. and Smith, S. (1989) 'Has Britain an early school-leaving problem?', *Fiscal Studies*, **10**, 1, 2–16.

Ministry of Education (1959) *15 to 18*, report for the Ministry of Education by the Central Advisory Council for Education Vol 1 (The Crowther Report), London: HMSO.

Mortimore, J., Mortimore, P. and Chitty, C. (1988) *Secondary School Examinations*, Bedford Way Papers No.18, revised edn, London: University of London.

Moser, C., Sir (1990) 'Our need for an informed society', 1990 Presidential Address to the British Association.

MSC (1982) *Youth Task Group Report* ,London: Manpower Services Commission.

MSC/DES (1986) *Review of Vocational Qualifications in England and Wales. A Report by the Working Group*, London: HMSO.

NCC (1990a) *Core Skills 16–19*, York: National Curriculum Council.

NCC (1990b) *Careers Education and Guidance, Curriculum Guidance 6*, York: National Curriculum Council.

NCVQ (1989a) *Generic Units and Common Learning Outcomes*, London: NCVQ.

NCVQ (1989b) *The NVQ Criteria and Related Guidance* , London: NCVQ.

NCVQ (1990a) *An Introduction to the National Record*, London: NCVQ.

NCVQ (1990b) *Common Learning Outcomes: Core Skills in A/AS Levels and NVQs*, London: NCVQ.

NCVQ (1991) *General National Vocational Qualifications: Proposals for the New Qualifications A Consultation Paper*, London: NCVQ.

NEDO (1988) *Young People and the Labour Market: A Challenge for the 1990s*, London: NEDO/Training Commission.

NEDO (1989) *Defusing the Demographic Timebomb*, London: NEDO.

Nettleship, J. (1990) 'Core skills and A/AS level', *Economics in Education*, Winter.

Norfolk County Council (1981) *One Year Courses 16+. Report of Chief Education Officer Review Group*, Norfolk County Council.

Pollard, A., Purvis, J and Walford, G. (eds.) (1988) *Education, Training and the New Vocationalism: Experience and Policy*, Milton Keynes: Open University Press.

Porter, M. (1990) *The Competitive Advantage of Nations*, Basingstoke: Macmillan.

Prais, S.J. (1981) 'Vocational training of the labour force in Britain and Germany', *National Institute Economic Review*, **98**, 47–59.

Prais, S.J. and Wagner, K. (1983) 'Some practical aspects of human capital investment: training standards in five occupations in Britain and Germany', *National Institute Economic Review*, **105**, 46–66.

Raffe, D. (1984) 'School attainment and the labour market', in Raffe, D. (ed.) *Fourteen to Eighteen: The Changing Pattern of Schooling in Scotland*, Aberdeen: Aberdeen University Press.

Raffe, D. (1985) 'Content and context' in Watts, A. (ed.) *Education and Training for 14–18 Year Olds: Policy and Practice*, Cambridge: NICEC.

Raffe, D. (1988) 'The story so far: research on education, training and the labour market from the Scottish surveys', in Raffe, D. (ed.) *Education and the Youth Labour Market: Schooling and Scheming*, London: Falmer Press.

Raffe, D. (1990) 'The transition from YTS to work: content, context and the external labour market', pp.52–73, in Wallace, C. and Cross, M. (eds.) *Youth in Transition: The Sociology of Youth and Youth Policy*, London: Falmer Press.

Rainbird, H. and Maguire, M. (1991) *Institutional Determinants of Adult Training*, ESRC End of Award Report.

Rainbow, B. (1990) 'The Wessex Project: Post-16 modular developments', in Hodkinson, P. (ed.) *TVEI and the Post-16 Curriculum*, Exeter: Wheaton Education.

Ranson, S., Taylor, B. and Brighouse, T. (1986) *The Revolution in Education and Training*, Harlow: Longman.

Reid, W.A. (1991) 'The ideology of access in comparative perspective', in Chitty, C. (ed.) *Post-16 Education: Studies in Access and Achievement,* London: Kogan Page.

Roberts, K., Dench, S. and Richardson, D. (1986) *The Changing Structure of Youth Labour Markets,* Research Paper 59, London: Department of Employment.

Royal Society (1991) *Beyond GCSE,* London: Royal Society.

RSA (Royal Society of Arts) (1991) *Learning Pays: The Role of Post-compulsory Education and Training,* London: RSA.

Ruddiman, K. (1990)'Search for the core', *Education,* **175**, 14, 346–7.

Ryan, P. (ed.) (1991) *International Comparisons of Vocational Education and Training for Intermediate Skills,* London: Falmer Press.

Saunders, C. (1991) 'Post-16 needs radical reform', *Times Higher Education Supplement,* 10 May 1991.

Saunders, M. (1985) *Emerging Issues in TVEI Implementation,* University of Lancaster.

Saunders, M., Fuller, A. and Lobley, D. (1990) *Emerging Issues in the Utilization of NVQs,* R&D Report 5, London: NCVQ.

Schools Council (1966) *Sixth-Form Curriculum and Examinations,* Working Paper 5, London: HMSO.

Schools Council (1972) *16–19 Growth and Response. 1. Curricular Bases,* Schools Council Working Party 45, London: Evans.

SEAC (1989a) *Report of the Findings of the Consultation on the Promotion of AS Examinations and the Rationalisation of A Level Syllabuses,* July, London: SEAC.

SEAC (1989b) *Advancing A Levels: A Response by the School Examinations and Assessment Council,* August, London: SEAC.

SEAC (1990a) *Examinations Post-16: Developments for the 1990s,* London: SEAC.

SEAC (1990b) *Letter to John MacGregor, 26 July 1990,* London: SEAC.

SEAC (1991a) *Report on the Consultation on Draft Principles for GCE A and AS Examinations,* London: SEAC.

SEAC (1991b) *European Colloquium,* London: SEAC.

Selby, D. (1989) 'Learning styles, learning needs', *Perspectives,* October.

SHA (1989) *16–19, The Way Forward,* Leicester: SHA.

Shackleton, J. (1988) 'The professional role of the lecturer', in FEU, *Planning the FE Curriculum: Implications of the 1988 Education Reform Act,* London: FEU.

Shelton, I. (1990) 'Social science in the curriculum', *Social Science Teacher,* **20**, 1.

Simon, B. (1981) 'Why no pedagogy in England?', in Simon, B. and Taylor, W. (eds.) *Education in the Eighties – The Central Issues,* London: Batsford.

Skilbeck, M., Lowe, N. and Tait, K. (1985) *A Question of Quality,* London: Institute of Education.

Smithers, A. (1991) *The Vocational Route into Higher Education,* University of

Manchester.

Smithers, A. and Robinson, P. (1989) *Increasing Participation in Higher Education*, Wetherby: BP.

Spencer, P. (1990) 'Aspects of entitlement', *West Midlands TVE Post 16 Network*, Autumn Newsletter.

Squirrell, G. (1991) *Youth Development Project Directory*, Sheffield: Employment Department.

Stansbury, D. (1975) *The Development of a New Curriculum Activator in Secondary Schools*, Devon: RPE Publications.

Stanton, G. (1990a) *Core Skills: Notes on Future FEU Action*, London: FEU.

Stanton, G. (1990b) Speech at TVEI Conference, Birmingham, March.

Steedman, H. (1990) 'Improvements in workplace qualifications: Britain and France 1979–88', *National Institute Economic Review*, 133, 50–61.

Steedman, H. and Wagner K. (1989) 'Productivity, machinery and skills: clothing manufacture in Britain and Germany', *National Institute Economic Review*, 128, 40–57.

Steedman, H., Mason, G. and Wagner, K. (1991) 'Intermediate skills in the workplace: deployment, standards and supply in Britain, France and Germany', *National Institute Economic Review*, 136, 60–76.

TA (1989) *Enterprise in Higher Education: Key Features of the Enterprise in Higher Education Projects 1988–89*, Sheffield: Training Agency.

TEED Higher Education Branch (1990) *Higher Education Developments: The Skills Link*, Sheffield: TEED.

TES (1990a) 'Employers' self-interest could blight common core', *Times Educational Supplement*, 13 April.

TES (1990b) 'No quickfix for training', *Times Educational Supplement*, June.

TES (1991) 'GVQs', *Times Educational Supplement*, 31 May.

Thompson, P. (1991) 'NVQs in the 1990s', *Educational Management and Administration*, 19, 2, 100–105.

TUC (1989) *Skills 2000*, London: TUC.

Turbin, J. (1987) State Intervention into the Labour Market for Youth The Implementation of the Youth. Training Scheme in Three Local Labour Markets, dissertation submitted for the degree of Ph.D., University of Leicester.

TVEI (1991) *Insight*, Sheffield: Employment Department, Unemployment Unit

Vincent, D. and Dean, J. (1977) *One Year Courses in Colleges and Sixth Form*, Slough: NFER.

Warwickshire LEA (1989) *The 16–19 Curriculum: A Discussion Paper*, Warwickshire LEA.

Waterhouse, P. (1983) *Supported Self Study. A Handbook for Teachers*, London: Council for Educational Technology.

Waterhouse, P. (1990) *Flexible Learning: An Outline*, Bath: Network Educational Press.

Welsh Office (1982) *Planning for Progress*, London: HMSO.

Whiteside, M.T. (1990) *Records of Achievement Post 16: The Management of Change. An Evaluation Report*, Northamptonshire LEA/University of Leicester

156

School of Education.

Wiener, M.J. (1981) *English Culture and the Decline of the Industrial Spirit 1850–1980,* Cambridge: Cambridge University Press.

Wigan Education Department (1990) *Higher Education and Records of Achievement. A Conference Report*, Metropolitan Borough of Wigan Education Department.

Wolf, A. (1990) 'Assessing Core Skills: Wisdom or Wild Goose Chase?', unpublished paper, Institute of Education, University of London.

Wood, D. (1991) 'Core Skills in 16-19 Education', unpublished paper, University of Leicester, School of Education.

Young, Lord (1990) *The Enterprise Years: A Businessman in the Cabinet,* London: Headline Book Publishers.

Youthaid (1992) *Working Brief,* March, London: Unemployment Unit and Youthaid.

Name Index

Ainley, P.   5, 20, 49, 52.
Anderson, E.   50.
Ashton, D. N.   24, 98-99, 103
Avis, J.   94.

Ball, C.   4, 12, 18, 20, 45, 48-49, 50, 79.
Baines, P.   78.
Baker, K.   12, 25, 35,46-47, 86-87, 137.
Barnett, C.   4, 105.
Barnes, D.   105.
Boffy, R.   34, 91
Broadfoot, P.   76-77, 80, 83.
Burrage, H.   89.
Bynner, J.   25.

Chitty, C.   22, 49.
Clarke, K.   7-8,13-14, 22, 35, 137.
Coates, P.   92, 94
Coffield, F.   20, 99.
Corney, M.   5.
Cresson, E.   23.

Dale, R.   4.
Dean, J.   55.
Duffy, M.   47.

Edwards, A.   43, 54.

Eggar, T.   62.

Finegold, D.   10, 14, 19-20, 24, 48, 111, 131.
Fitzgibbon, C.   113.

Gleeson, D   4, 78.
Gretton, R.   83.
Guthrie, J. W.   7.

Haffenden, I.   51.
Halsey, P.   87.
Hargreaves, A   49.
Harland, J.   43, 51, 104.
Hayes, C.   6, 13, 21.
Holness,M.   89.
Holt, M.   4.
House, E. R.   65, 74.

Jackson, R.   6, 12, 44.
Jarvis, V.   10, 13, 24.
Jessup, G.   13, 38.
Jewell, D.   48.
Johnson, R.   21.
Jones, A.   65, 79.
Jones, K.   52-53, 94.

Knight, C.   22.

Law, B.   77.

158

Subject Index

162